THOMAS JEFFERSON

THEN AND NOW

1743 — 1943

A NATIONAL SYMPOSIUM

Edited by

JAMES WATERMAN WISE

Issued by

BILL OF RIGHTS SESQUI - CENTENNIAL COMMITTEE

17 EAST 42ND STREET, NEW YORK

1943

BILL OF RIGHTS

SESQUI-CENTENNIAL COMMITTEE

Honorary Chairman
FRANKLIN DELANO ROOSEVELT

Honorary Vice-Chairmen
JAMES M. COX
JOHN W. DAVIS
HERBERT HOOVER
ALF M. LANDON
SAM RAYBURN
ALFRED E. SMITH
HENRY A. WALLACE
WENDELL WILLKIE

National Chairman
HERBERT BAYARD SWOPE

National Secretary
JAMES WATERMAN WISE

NATIONAL COMMITTEE

Helen C. White, *President*, AMERICAN ASSOCIATION OF UNIVERSITY WOMEN

Mrs. G. Walter Williams, *Past National President*, AMERICAN GOLD STAR MOTHERS

Mrs. Irving Fairweather, *National President*, AMERICAN WAR MOTHERS

Walter W. Head, *President*, BOY SCOUTS OF AMERICA

Martha F. Allen, *National Executive*, CAMP FIRE GIRLS

Mary C. Duffy, *Supreme Regent*, CATHOLIC DAUGHTERS OF AMERICA

Joseph Berning, *Supreme President*, THE CATHOLIC KNIGHTS OF AMERICA

Raymond Gram Swing, *Honorary Chairman*, COUNCIL FOR DEMOCRACY

Laurence R. Melton, *National Commander*, DISABLED AMERICAN VETERANS OF THE WORLD WAR

Samuel McCrea Cavert, *General Secretary*, THE FEDERAL COUNCIL OF THE CHURCHES OF CHRIST IN AMERICA

E. Mark Sullivan, *Grand Exalted Ruler*, GRAND LODGE, BENEVOLENT AND PROTECTIVE ORDER OF ELKS

Charles H. Johnson, *Grand Secretary*, GRAND LODGE FREE AND ACCEPTED MASONS, NEW YORK STATE

Benjamin Kaufman, *National Commander*, JEWISH WAR VETERANS OF THE UNITED STATES

Francis P. Matthews, *Supreme Knight*, KNIGHTS OF COLUMBUS

James J. Davis, *Director General*, LOYAL ORDER OF MOOSE

Walter White, *Secretary*, NATIONAL ASSOCIATION FOR THE ADVANCEMENT OF COLORED PEOPLE

Mrs. Maurice L. Goldman, *President*, NATIONAL COUNCIL OF JEWISH WOMEN

A. C. Flora, *President*, NATIONAL EDUCATION ASSOCIATION OF THE UNITED STATES

Joe Hanley, *Commander-in-Chief*, UNITED SPANISH WAR VETERANS

Robert B. Handy, Jr., *Adjutant General*, VETERANS OF FOREIGN WARS OF THE UNITED STATES

Eugene Barnett, *General Secretary*, NATIONAL COUNCIL, YOUNG MEN'S CHRISTIAN ASSOCIATION

Louis M. Loeb, *Acting President*, YOUNG MEN'S HEBREW ASSOCIATION

Mrs. Henry A. Ingraham, *President*, NATIONAL BOARD, YOUNG WOMEN'S CHRISTIAN ASSOCIATIONS

Mrs. Ruth Reutlinger, *Executive Director*, YOUNG WOMEN'S HEBREW ASSOCIATION

TABLE OF CONTENTS

TABLE OF CONTENTS

FOREWORD

MR. THOMAS JEFFERSON—and the Mister became a part of his title because he fought so hard against "Your Majesty" being used for the President—is one of the elements in America's Trinity, with George Washington and Abraham Lincoln.

Jefferson profoundly affected the other two. Lincoln's political philosophy, in fact, was almost wholly Jeffersonian. He was the chief disciple of America's Apostle of Liberty.

This foreword and the writings of the distinguished men and women which follow are efforts to bring Jefferson home to the people who owe him so much.

But no matter how magic the words of others may be they are less than the words of the man himself. Through him we know him.

So I group here some of the phrases he spoke and acted on. They reveal his measure as nothing else can. He wrote in the immortal Declaration of Independence:

"We hold these truths to be self-evident: that all men are created equal; that they are endowed by their Creator with certain inalienable rights; among these are life, liberty and the pursuit of happiness; that to secure these rights governments are instituted among men. We . . . solemnly publish and declare that these colonies are and of right ought to be free and independent states. . . . and for the support of this declaration, with a firm reliance on the protection of Divine Providence, we mutually pledge our lives, our fortunes and our sacred honor."

7

His influence in the formation of the Constitution and his authorship of the Bill of Rights (the first ten amendments dealing with Human Rights) are well known. Concerning one of these rights, he said:

"Almighty God hath created the mind free. All attempts to influence it by temporal punishments or burthens . . . are a departure from the plan of the Holy Author of our religion. . . . No man shall be compelled to frequent or support any religious worship or ministry or shall otherwise suffer on account of his religious opinions or belief; but all men shall be free to profess, and by argument to maintain, their opinions in matters of religion. I know but one code of morality for men whether acting singly or collectively."

Against Conservatism he spoke thus:

"I am not an advocate for frequent changes in laws and constitutions, but laws and institutions must go hand in hand with the progress of the human mind. As that becomes more developed, more enlightened, as new discoveries are made, new truths discovered and manners and opinions change, institutions must advance also to keep pace with the times. We might as well require a man to wear still the coat which fitted him when a boy as civilized society to remain ever under the regimen of their barbarous ancestors."

He epitomized his thinking in this way:

"I have sworn on the Altar of God eternal hostility to every form of tyranny over the mind of man."

Jefferson saw 140 years ago the nature and force of our alliance with Great Britain. "We must marry ourselves to the British Fleet and Nation," he declared.

He urged "the union of the two nations who, in conjunction, can maintain exclusive control of the ocean. . . . This is not a state of affairs we seek or desire. It is one forced on us as necessary. . . . by the laws of nature. . . ."

In working with the other English speaking nation, Jefferson, never an Anglo-phile, emphasized the fact that such cooperation with Britain, in order to strengthen the young North and South American democracies, would be "to maintain our own principles, not to depart from them." This was part of the advice that helped to bring the Monroe Doctrine into being.

The precept was uttered at a time when the ring of "no entangling alliances" was still in the ears of the struggling people. The myth of safety through isolation dies hard. But it is dying. There lies the great hope for the future peace of the world!

Today Peace is our danger—not our goal. We seek Victory not a truce.

The life of this man helps in all of the phases of our fight.

His statute for Religious Freedom in Virginia was a leap into the future—so far that some have not caught up to him yet.

Jefferson brought us the territory that lay in the Louisiana Purchase and the Lewis and Clark Northwest Expedition. But he did more. He trusted the people and they rose to that trust. He fired them, through his spirit of selflessness, with a passion against injustice and a devotion to liberty. He gave them dignity and made them proud to be Americans—a title that millions went through hardship to gain. He made the land a sanctuary, and those who found refuge here have played their part in making the country great. They, too, "have refreshed the Tree of Liberty with the blood of patriots and tyrants."

In Public Opinion lies the final political power, Jefferson taught, and all the world accepts that truth. Its application is tortured and bedevilled in tyrannies. Even the antichrist, Hitler, uses the system. But that won't be for long!

One more of his revelatory and prophetic utterances —it could have been written yesterday:

"When we reflect that the eyes of the virtuous all over earth are turned with anxiety on us, as the only depositories of the sacred fire of liberty, and that our falling into anarchy would decide forever the destinies of mankind, and seal the political heresy that man is incapable of self-government, the only contest between divided friends should be who will dare farthest into the ranks of the common enemy."

Jefferson left none of his name. Like Washington, his heritage belongs to the people. While the Republic lives, Jefferson will not be forgotten.

Mr. Jefferson died as the bells tolled the Golden (fiftieth) Anniversary of his great work—the Declaration of Independence—on July 4, 1826.

He could not have chosen a better requiem.

—HERBERT BAYARD SWOPE, *Chairman,*
Bill of Rights Sesqui-Centennial Committee

10

THE FIRST EMANCIPATOR

IT IS INDEED MOST FITTING that not only we in America, but everyone everywhere who believes in the emancipation of the spirit of man should take the opportunity afforded by this occasion—the celebration of the 200th anniversary of Thomas Jefferson's birth—to dedicate ourselves anew to the basic principles which he set forth of the Four Freedoms — Liberty, Freedom, Equality and Justice.

This country, in the course of a great and eventful history, that has brought to mankind everywhere the hope of eternal freedom, which has served through the years as a beacon light to liberty-loving people the world over, has produced men of great stature. In the early formative stages of this great nation—days that tried the souls of man—there rose above the great body of the people one who shall always be immortalized in our hearts as the first Emancipator—Thomas Jefferson.

With the forces of hate and destruction unloosed upon the frontiers of the world, it is more essential now than ever before that we in America should stand and fight for the principles and philosophy of government which have been handed down through the years by that great American, and the father of democracy, Thomas Jefferson.

The battles of today's globular war are being fought for the Four Freedoms which were given the world by Thomas Jefferson when he wrote the American Declaration of Independence. His outstanding performance as a public official exemplified those principles which he so ardently advocated perhaps more than has been so in the case of any other servant of the people.

Not only Americans, but all who believe that the soul and spirit of man must remain free must guard the ramparts against those who would seek to destroy the philosophy of government this great man has given to the world.

—W. WARREN BARBOUR,
United States Senator

A PATTERN FOR THE FUTURE

MORE THAN AT ANY PREVIOUS TIME in our history Thomas Jefferson's philosophy is an important living thing for Americans. On the surface, it may occasionally appear that Jefferson's creed is somewhat outmoded; we are a long way from the simple pastoral society with which Jefferson was most familiar, and our social system, our economic system and our Government are all much more complex and formalized than anything he contemplated. Nevertheless, all of this is merely a surface change. The underlying significance of the Jeffersonian ideal is even more timely today than it was when this republic was young and was still making its own pattern.

For, although this country has changed profoundly since Jefferson's day, it is still setting a pattern for the future; and largely because the Jeffersonian ideal has worked like a ferment throughout the country during all of these years, a good part of the hopes of mankind are still bound up in the kind of pattern which we set for ourselves. The conditions under which we live are different, but the problem remains the same—to perfect on this continent a human society which will give to its individual members the greatest possible opportunity to live and grow with a maximum of freedom and under restraints which are self-imposed and not imposed by circumstances or by arbitrary law. The very fact that conditions have changed so greatly—that the mechanics of living in a large and complex system have narrowed the individual's area of freedom in so many respects—makes it supremely important that we continue to understand that the basic meaning of America remains today what it was in Jefferson's own time: liberty for each man to make the most, according to his own lights, of whatever talents, capabilities and ideals he finds in his own heart.

—W. L. BATT,
Vice Chairman, War Production Board

JEFFERSON'S PROPHETIC VISION

IN THE MIDST OF WAR it is altogether right that the fighting people should, from time to time, remember their dead statesmen and soldiers. For they are the symbols that give continuity to the ideals of the nation, whose acts belong as of right to the nation, and to the men and women of the nation. So that, after many years, when the country is threatened and its future challenged, we identify ourselves with our great dead, to feel in our hearts the continuity of their greatness, a very part of our history and national heritage.

Two hundred years ago today Thomas Jefferson was born. He had come to full manhood when the American Colonies determined they could no longer remain a part of the Kingdom of Great Britain where they were not free men according to their views of what freedom meant. In declaring the independence of the thirteen states, in uniting them, in expanding their territory and their power, and above all in defining the bases of their ideals, Jefferson took his place among the great founding fathers.

Those early American ideals are now a part of our national assumptions. Whenever they are, or may be, threatened we are prepared to fight. Universal education, freedom of the press, a state divorced from any church, political equality—these things that Jefferson so splendidly supported—are now the essence of our way of living. He hated and feared the concentration of power in the hands of the few, and knew that no democracy could survive where the practices of the government had been either delegated by the people beyond their participation, or usurped by tyrants and dictators.

He is therefore today a living symbol of the things Americans cherish. Now that we are fighting to preserve these things, challenged elsewhere so universally, the memory of Thomas Jefferson renews our faith and our strength to achieve the perpetuation of all the democratic rights for which the revolution was fought. What he once said about our democracy shows his prophetic vision of its universal aspects. "A nation," he said, "composed of such materials, and free in all its members from distressing wants, furnishes hopeful implements for the interesting experiment of self-government; and we feel that we are acting under obligations not confined to the limits of our own society. It is impossible not to be sensible that we are acting for all mankind; that circumstances denied to others, but indulged to us, have imposed on us the duty of proving what is the degree of freedom and self-government in which a society may venture to leave its individual members."

—FRANCIS BIDDLE,
Attorney General of the United States

CRUSADER AGAINST IGNORANCE

THE NATIONWIDE CELEBRATION of the birthday of Thomas Jefferson bids one to think what manner of man he was that two hundred years after his birth and more than one hundred and thirty years after he retired from public life the whole nation celebrates his birth.

He was a leader among the founders of our republic, a rare group of men, many of them had fought in our army, and others who had done equally valiant service with their tongues and pens and shared the danger of leaders of rebellion.

When Richard Henry Lee of Virginia moved in the third Continental Congress that "Independence be declared", Jefferson was appointed chairman of a committee of five to write the proper resolution to be adopted, and was asked by the committee to write the declaration himself. That famous Declaration of Independence we celebrate every year on Independence Day.

Throughout his life Thomas Jefferson worked for justice, for equality of opportunity. He is called the spiritual father of the Bill of Rights, for many of the rights given in those first ten amendments to our Constitution, through his efforts had already been given to the people of his State (Virginia), during his years as member of the House of Burgesses and as Governor of Virginia.

These messages of appreciation of the life and character of Thomas Jefferson will be sent widely to schools, for that reason attention should be called especially to his ardent work for public education.

Let him speak again in the following quotations from some of his letters:

"I think by far the most important bill in our whole code is that for the diffusion of knowledge among the people. No other sure foundation can be devised for the preservation of freedom and happiness. . . . Preach, my dear Sir, a crusade against ignorance; establish and improve the law for educating the common people.

"Every government degenerates when trusted to the rulers of the people alone. The people themselves therefore are its only safe depositories. And to render them safe, their minds must be improved to a certain degree. . . . An amendment of our Constitution must here come in aid of public education. The influence over government must be shared by all the people.

"A bill of rights is what the people are entitled to against every government on earth, general or particular, and what no just government should refuse or rest on inference."

When he retired at the end of his second term as President of the United States, it was largely to devote his time to the superintendence of the University of Virginia, for the establishment of which he had been mainly responsible, and to which he had given generously.

Let our schools celebrate him as a leader in education as the "foundation for the preservation of freedom and happiness."

—KATHERINE DEVEREUX BLAKE

WHAT THE WORLD NEEDS TODAY

THE NAME AND LIFE WORK OF THOMAS JEFFERSON were never more important than they are at the moment. In his life time he was the outstanding exponent of civil, economic and religious liberty. He had the vision of a prophet and the sagacity of a trained and highly experienced statesman. Those fundamental doctrines of human freedom and individual liberty upon which he insisted and which he taught both in this country and in Europe during the whole of his life and which we believe to be essential to a continuing and liberty-loving civilization are now assailed as they never have been before. We are told by ambitious and power-loving despots, apparently with seriousness, that the doctrines of Jefferson are not only untrue and unwise but that they must not be read or debated or even talked about. They are on the proscribed list of ideas and ideals in countries whose people are under emotional and political control of despots. No better service could be rendered to mankind at this time or in the years immediately to follow than to emphasize over and over again Jefferson's ideals and the methods by which he proposed to achieve them.

There can be no substitute for individual liberty.

Collective action and administration if freely controlled by individuals for whose interests it exists is practicable and wise, but collective control of individuals by organized groups in the interest of those groups whether they seek power or profit is impossible in a society of free men.

We should celebrate the name and the life of Thomas Jefferson not only on his 200th birthday but wherever free men gather to express and to protect their freedom. This is the time to recall the famous statement of John Adams made on his death-bed when he did not know that Thomas Jefferson had already passed from earth, "Thomas Jefferson still lives." What the world most needs today is an Alexander Hamilton to organize it and a Thomas Jefferson to give it controlling principles and ideals.

—NICHOLAS MURRAY BUTLER,
President, Columbia University

APOSTLE OF HUMAN FREEDOM

FOR MORE THAN FIFTY YEARS Thomas Jefferson was a leader in American politics. Member of the Second Continental Congress and of Congress under the early Confederation, Governor of Virginia, minister to France; then Secretary of State, Vice-President, and President of the United States; later for seventeen years a revered counselor of the government and people of the young nation—small wonder his birthday is still celebrated and his monumental writings are still searched for authority as to the purposes of the founders of this republic.

It was during a period of great changes, in which the area of settlement spread from a narrow fringe along the Atlantic Coast beyond the Mississippi River, a period that witnessed the early development of the Industrial Revolution, that the gangling youth who had never seen a settlement of more than twenty houses before his seventeenth year matured through rich national and international experience into the Sage of Monticello. What message from that so distant voice and pen is valid today in this industrial civilization which had hardly begun to dawn in his time—which he could never have envisaged?

Many a message, it seems; for Jefferson is quoted today more than any other statesman of his time. His writings, spread over so many years and reflecting his sensitiveness to changing America and a changing world, furnish texts to both conservatives and liberals, to both reactionaries and radicals, to both Republicans and Democrats, in the present scene. To the end of his life his opinions on many subjects varied as his experience ripened—but as the foremost American apostle of democracy he never wavered in his fundamental faith in government of the people by and for themselves. It is enshrined in the Declaration of Independence, in the Bill of Rights, in his Presidential messages and papers, in his published letters. That unwavering faith is his greatest legacy.

It was to the end of establishing and maintaining democracy that he advocated wide extension of public education, proposed the provision for support of public schools that was included in the Land Ordinance of 1785, opposed centralization of power in the federal government, and upheld the "unalienable rights" of the individual. He kept his vow: "I have sworn before the altar of God eternal hostility against every form of tyranny over the mind of man." Dedicating his life to the service of freedom, he saw in the principles and processes of democracy the hope of humanity.

In our complex industrial society, the forms and institutions of effective democracy are bound to be different from what were practicable and desirable in pre-industrial America. We find the middle road between individual freedom and social control tortuous and difficult. Yet we shall do well to preserve Thomas Jefferson's faith and hope—faith that democracy is the only form of government under which an approximation to freedom and justice can be realized, and hope that through all the changes in human relationships we can make America more and more a land of opportunity for all its people.

—HOWARD COONLEY,
Former President,
National Association of Manufacturers

HIS DOMINANT PASSION

IN ESTIMATING the work and character of any man it is well to find out, if possible, what the man thought of himself, and of his most important achievements. In the case of Thomas Jefferson the evidence seems clear, for he wrote his own epitaph in this simple statement: "Author of the Declaration of American Independence, of the Statute of Virginia for Religious Freedom, and Father of the University of Virginia".

While some historians believe that Thomas Jefferson tops the list of all the American Presidents in mental equipment, it is evident that Jefferson did not consider his work as President of the United States his supreme achievement. To the end of his life he seemed sure that his supreme contribution was in connection with laying foundations that would stand against intolerance and for democratic freedom. Chosen with John Adams, Benjamin Franklin, Roger Sherman and Robert R. Livingston to draft a Declaration of Independence, it was Jefferson who did the actual writing, and that writing has changed the course of the history of the world.

In a letter which Jefferson wrote to a friend, at a time when he was himself a victim of political intolerance, he says, "If any doubt has arisen as to me, my Country will have my political creed, in the form of a 'Declaration' which I was lately directed (by the Continental Congress) to draw. This will give decisive proof that my own sentiment concurred with the vote they instructed us to give".

Thus it seems very evident that the present world conflict, for freedom from mental and physical enslavement, is but the continuation of that crusade for liberty, which was the dominant passion of Thomas Jefferson's life.

—RALPH SPAULDING CUSHMAN,
Methodist Bishop,
Saint Paul, Minnesota

OUR ONLY TIMELESS STATESMAN

THOMAS JEFFERSON is the one American statesman who is timeless. The truths he enunciated in the Declaration of Independence in 1776 contain lights to which men look out of darkened windows in 1943 yearning for their freedom. Lincoln better than anyone else comprehended the permanence and virtue of Jefferson's Declaration when he wrote that Jefferson "had the coolness, forecast and capacity to introduce into a merely revolutionary doctrine an abstract truth, applicable to all men and all times, and so to embalm it there that today, and in all coming days, it shall be a rebuke and a stumbling block to the very harbinger of reappearing tyranny."

It was the propaganda and pen of the Sage of Monticello which insured the incorporation of the Bill of Rights as the very heart of the Constitution.

It was Jefferson's crusade against the Alien and Sedition law which forever prevents legislation that imprisons editors who exercise the right to criticize public officials. "I am", he wrote, "for the freedom of the press and against all violations of the Constitution to silence by force and not by reason, the complaints or criticisms, just or unjust, of our citizens against the conduct of their agents."

It was the early resolve of Thomas Jefferson which ended the union of church and state, and undemocratic practices in his Virginia, and foreshadowed religious freedom and equality when the colonies became a republic by his authorship of the Statute of Religious Liberty in his Commonwealth.

It was the wisdom of Thomas Jefferson that Monroe drew upon in his promulgation of the Monroe Doctrine which preceded the Good Neighbor Policy.

It was devotion to learning and equality of opportunity that made Jefferson the founder of the University of Virginia, the mother of broad state-supported universities, free from any control less broad than that of the state, and of the plan of universal public education which has become the American pattern of instruction for all the children of the country. Jefferson held that "if the condition of man is to be progressively ameliorated, as we fondly hope and believe, education is to be the chief instrument in effecting it."

It was Thomas Jefferson who was the first statesman of the South to understand the dangers incident in human slavery and to wish it ended by gradual emancipation.

It was the pen of Thomas Jefferson which indicted King George for preventing desirable immigration to the colonies and his leadership which opened the doors to the entrance of desirable citizens out of all the European stocks, building here an American spirit which is the hope of mankind in all parts of the world.

It was the adventurous spirit of Thomas Jefferson

that sent Lewis and Clark on the expedition that built a republic from the Atlantic to the Pacific. It was the statesmanship of Thomas Jefferson that brought about the Louisiana Purchase, doubling the area of the United States, and controlling the navigation of the father of waters in this hemisphere.

It was Jefferson whose versatility made him equally at home as a dirt and scientific farmer, architect, scientist, inventor, author, parliamentarian, and the patron of all the arts and sciences and progress in every domain of government and improvement in living conditions. But his greatest contribution was his belief in the right and ability of the people to control their own destinies holding that "the people are the only sure reliance for the preservation of our liberty."

In Jefferson's day the call was for the freedoms set forth in the Bill of Rights. Our Four Freedoms are of the spirit of the early freedoms exhorted from Kings, but Freedom From Want and Freedom From Fear are the natural evolution of the Jefferson freedoms for all men everywhere, for all time.

—JOSEPHUS DANIELS,
*Former United States
Ambassador to Mexico*

ARMED WITH SUCH WEAPONS

ON THE TWO HUNDREDTH ANNIVERSARY of the birth of
Thomas Jefferson and at this particular crisis in the
affairs of the world it is worth while for every American
to consider what it was that Jefferson taught, to ask
himself whether he believes in his teachings and if so
whether he is ready to fight for them.

Some of the things Jefferson taught are these, which
I give without quotation marks but practically in his
own words; that God who gave us life gave us liberty
at the same time; mankind is possessed of certain inherent and inalienable rights among which are life,
liberty and the pursuit of happiness. Every man and
every body of men on earth have the right to self-
government; for if man cannot be trusted to govern
himself how can he be trusted to govern others. It is
not true that some men are born into the world with
saddles on their backs while others are born booted
and spurred to ride them legitimately by the grace of
God. The inconveniences attending too much liberty
are better than those attending too small a degree of it.
The foundation of republican government is the equal
right of every citizen in his person, in his property and
in their management. It's essence is action by the citi-

zens on matters within their right and competence and in all other matters by representatives chosen for that purpose. Education is the only sure foundation for the preservation of freedom and happiness. Our country is too large to have all its affairs directed by a single government, and it is therefore of immense consequence that the states retain as complete authority as possible over their own citizens. The aim of good government is equal and exact justice to all men of whatever state or persuasion, religious or political. A wise and frugal government which shall restrain men from injuring one another, shall leave them free to regulate their own pursuits of industry and improvement, and shall not take from the mouth of labor the bread it has earned—this is the sum of good government.

Throughout all his utterances there runs like a thread of purest gold his faith in the worth and dignity of each individual man. This is the essence of Jefferson's philosophy. Here is the mainspring of his every action; here the inspiration of his entire life and here the secret of his lasting influence on the lives of other Americans. It is this faith by which the mountains of caste and prejudice and privilege are moved, and before which tyranny and oppression well may tremble. Armed with such weapons as Jefferson forged lovers of freedom can still go forth conquering and to conquer.

This is not a new doctrine. It was not new in the days of Jefferson. Indeed, it has been the creed of all those lofty souls who aspired throughout the ages to be leaders and teachers of mankind. It found its supreme exponent in the Man of Galilee. Yet new or old it has never been without opponents and, thank God, has never lacked defenders ready to die if need be in its behalf. Around the world today the combat rages and over every ocean and continent the clarions of battle call. Can there be any doubt where America stands?

—JOHN W. DAVIS

WE FIGHT FOR EQUALITY

THE UNITED STATES, haven of freedom since its birth, is passing through the most critical period in its history. The world is embroiled in a war between freedom-loving people and the forces of slavery. It is peculiarly fitting that at such a time we should celebrate the 200th anniversary of the birth of Thomas Jefferson, one of the fathers of free government in North America.

In a period when each day calls for new sacrifices by our people and new limitations on the freedom we are fighting to preserve, the principles which Jefferson penned in the Declaration of Independence take on a fresh significance. What could more aptly describe the purposes for which we are fighting today than his immortal declaration "that all men are created equal, that they are endowed, by their Creator, with certain inalienable rights, that among these are life, liberty, and the pursuit of happiness."

The principles which inspired thirteen struggling colonies in 1776 today serve to rally the freedom-loving people of the entire world. The gallant band of American patriots who affixed their signatures to Jefferson's document, pledging to each other "our lives, our fortunes and our sacred honor," has grown to include free men everywhere in the United Nations who are ready to sacrifice their very lives for the dignity and freedom of man.

We have learned through blood and sacrifice that civilization is not possible in a world where an aggressor nation can attempt to annihilate a peace-loving people. We have learned that the principles which Jefferson declared were inherent to the rights of man are deserving of the widest application lest freedom everywhere be imperiled.

We will have been untrue to the spirit of Jefferson—we will have failed in our great objective—, unless we come out of this war with new and greater freedom. We must wipe out the intolerance and bigotry which still stand in the way of the full enjoyment of the freedom and opportunity guaranteed to all our people. We must banish from the face of the earth the poisonous concept of race superiority.

With the end of this war, that equality of man which Jefferson envisaged will be extended, God willing, to the Jewish Rabbi in Warsaw, the Catholic Priest in Vienna, the Pastor Niemollers who languish in concentration camps, the Chinese peasant, the Negro sharecropper—in short, to all who are downtrodden and underprivileged. Without it freedom cannot hope to survive.

—THOMAS E. DEWEY,
Governor of New York

THE FOREMOST AMERICAN

THE VISITOR TO Independence Hall, Philadelphia, looking at the high chair behind the table upon which the Declaration of Independence was signed, is no longer uncertain whether the insignia of the sun carved thereon is a rising sun or a setting sun. Benjamin Franklin exclaimed that he long wondered which it was; but the adoption of this Declaration written by Thomas Jefferson and proposed by him to the Continental Congress then in session, fixed the fact that it was a rising sun.

The Continental Congress by adoption of this Declaration made Freedom under Democracy the American ideal. Thus the great work of Jefferson became the fundamental principle of the new nation. Adopted by the thirteen Colonies in 1776 it has since been established in all of the American Republics. It has been accepted by one nation after another until eventually it will include all the nations of the world.

Thomas Jefferson is thus established as the foremost American. The Founder fathers of our nation accepted his creed. Washington and Franklin were followers of the Jeffersonian idea. One led the American armies to victory dedicated to its fulfillment. The other promulgated its doctrine at home and foreign lands. The adoption of the Federal Constitution and its Bill of Rights naturally followed, thus guaranteeing the protection of this fundamental principle in established law.

Thus became the active recognition of the most fundamental of human rights—the right to freedom and the equality of man. These rights being dependent neither on sex, race, religion, or abode; the equality of each individual before the law; the equal responsibility under the law. It is upon this principle that justice is founded and with justice—peace, security, and the happiness of mankind is to be secured. Freedom under Democracy is the American ideal—the rising sun of the universe of today, of tomorrow, and forever.

The great war in which the nations of the world are now engaged will determine whether this Jeffersonian principle is to continue or to perish. It will end in its universal acceptance.

It must not be forgotten that Jefferson expounded the Christian doctrine of the independence and dignity of man, and put into practical form in government the great spiritual truth expressed by the Saviour of mankind. Jefferson was the great apostle of Democracy. He sought to make men free. His country became the promised land of Freedom. Its expanding power and influence will make permanent his great principle for the eternal happiness of mankind. Jefferson's name will remain ever secure while Freedom lasts.

—MICHAEL FRANCIS DOYLE

THE WORLD'S BEST HOPE

THE TEMPTATION to indulge in an emotional, patriotic eulogy by stating that Thomas Jefferson was, and is, the creator of our "brave new world" would be given the lie by his own words. He said that the object of the Declaration of Independence was "not to find out new principles or new arguments never before thought of . . . but to place before mankind the common sense of the subject, in terms so plain and firm as to command their assent. . . . It was intended to be an expression of the American mind."

The use of the phrase *"place before mankind"* should be noted. He was an international nationalist. He did not feel that patriotism was incompatible with efforts to insure world peace and justice as, for instance, when he proposed "to marry the British Fleet."

Just as today, Hitler is the evil reflection of an evil condition existing in his community, so was Jefferson the glorious reflection of a glorious condition existing in *his* community. Disruptive forces existed then as now but the roots of the civilization represented by Jefferson were wholesome. His insistence on the Right, as he saw it, was stubborn and uncompromising, as Hamilton learned and admitted. But it was not so myopic as to prevent his writing a plea for mediation and collaboration in one of the most moving but least known documents of the time, called "The Olive Branch Petition," only a few months before the Declaration. He was able to view things in their proper proportion without becoming detached from the issue at hand.

His influence *was* great because he possessed the ability not just to express *himself* but to express the deep convictions of "the American mind" and of the mind of *all* free men. He was not just a product of the age—he was a product of the *Ages*. He was the instrument through which centuries of political conviction and theory were crystalized and adapted to the problems of his era.

His influence *is* great because of the breadth and integrity of his basic ideals. Yet not all of the Jeffersonian conceptions of life are applicable to our day. He was opposed to industrialism in all its manifestations. Democracy as we think of it today had not yet become an issue in his time of limited suffrage and slavery. But he should not lose stature because certain aspects of our society have changed since then. His primary concern, which was for the freedom and the dignity and the happiness of man, is still today the guiding aspiration of our people. The unequivocal terms by which he restated men's rights created fresh determination in all peoples, particularly in those who had enjoyed a tradition of freedom. He was the American reincarnation of the spirit which set down the Magna Charta.

The design of our system may *appear* to vary from time to time but so long as free men live, those principles which guided the philosophy of Thomas Jefferson and which influence us, remain the indestructible and immortal skeleton of our body politic. The ideals which were the foundations of our form of government have undergone no change. And despite differences over methods, the objectives of all democratic peoples today still sustain Jefferson's belief that the framework by which we govern ourselves "is the world's best hope."

—DOUGLAS FAIRBANKS, JR.,
Lieutenant, U.S.N.R.

JEFFERSON—THE MAN

OTHERS CONTRIBUTING to this collection of statements
about Thomas Jefferson will certainly bring out both
his incomparable services to the cause of democracy,
and the constantly increasing appreciation by Americans of these services in the political field. They can
scarcely be overstated. The first forty years of our nation's life would be unimaginable to us without
Thomas Jefferson. But since, in the coming national
celebration of the 200th anniversary of Jefferson's
birth, his towering political greatness will be recalled
to all our minds, it may be permitted to one of his ad-
mirers to express something of the warm affection his
countrymen feel for the enchanting personality of this
red-headed, interesting, humorous, friendly lover of
human life. His is, is it not, with that of Benjamin
Franklin's, the only lovable, interesting and fascinat-
ing personality among all those noble men of our early
history?

Let it not be forgotten by Americans, profoundly
grateful for Jefferson's integrity, for the bold beauty of
his conception of democracy, for his notable gifts as a
writer, and his example of untiring courageous devotion to his country's interests, that he set another exam-

ple to all of us, hardly less vital to our welfare; the example of heartily enjoying normal human existence for all the long years he experienced it. He had his fair share and more, of grief, disappointment, unfair attacks, struggle against embittered adversaries, money difficulties. But his sweet-tempered, sunny, affectionate nature, his insatiable intellectual curiosity, his zestful interest in all the phenomena of growth, mental, spiritual, biological, all protected him from the disillusioned revulsion which saddens so many fine personalities in their middle and later years. It would be literally impossible for any of us to imagine Thomas Jefferson false to a trust, cruel, cowardly, or dishonest. It is as impossible to imagine him bored, bitter, or resentful. The thought of Jefferson the patriot, is for all Americans, a bugle-call to duty. The thought of Jefferson the man, is sunshine in a shady place.

—Dorothy Canfield Fisher

MORAL AND SPIRITUAL IDEALS

CRITICAL TIMES CALL FOR and demand a restudy of the footings that constitute our chief security. This is more true of a young and signally prospered nation than of those whose roots go into the remote past. America as an experiment in government traces its lineage to those men who, over one hundred and fifty years ago, planned its course, gave it its sailing orders in the form of a Constitution and Bill of Rights, and set it on its way to high accomplishment. The leaders or architects of this great experiment were men of commanding stature. They were men of sound learning and most of them were comparatively young. Certain of them were range-finders, careful yet daring, who knew the kind of government they wished to found, gifted in vision, strong of will and purpose.

Among the outstanding of these younger men was Thomas Jefferson. Possessed of a fine mind with an amazing genius for registering his thoughts, coupled with undaunted courage, he filled a conspicuous niche in this galaxy of great men. The influence he exercised in the shaping of our fundamental law was greater possibly than that of his colleagues. Others will give him high praise for the large part he played in the

Constitutional Convention. I venture a word concerning his deep moral and religious convictions. Too often this is forgotten. Some of his critics have regarded him as a refined pagan, steeped in the classics, whose fine phrases color his writings. Let him speak for himself. In comparing Plato, Aristotle, Socrates and others with the Son of man, he says: "The precepts of the ancient philosophers related chiefly to ourselves, and the government of those passions which, unrestrained, would disturb our tranquility of mind. In this branch of philosophy they were really great. Their ideas of God and of His attributes were degrading and injurious. Their system was Deism. Their ethics were not only imperfect, but often irreconcilable with the sound dictates of reason and morality." Turning to Christ, he wrote: "His moral doctrines, relating to kindred and friends, were more pure and perfect than those of the most correct of the philosophers. He pushed His scrutinies into the heart of man; erected His tribunal in the region of His thoughts and purified the waters of the fountain-head. He taught emphatically, the doctrine of a future state, and wielded it with efficiency, as an important incentive, supplementary to the other motives to moral conduct."

This brief excerpt is worthy of our reflection as we contemplate his lofty place among the founding fathers of the Republic. The sheer massiveness of the contribution he made to the shaping of our government cannot be lost sight of at this momentous period in our history, nor may we estimate lightly the strong moral and spiritual ideals that motivated him. Under the stress of a titanic struggle that involves our most precious institutions, it is well that we "look unto the rock whence we are hewn," and seek to follow the well-charted course, in the making of which, Thomas Jefferson played so large a part. Praise him we will, emulate his virtues and his loyalty to truth we must. Laws and statutes have their essential place in government, but government without moral and spiritual ideals cannot endure.

—JAMES E. FREEMAN,
Bishop of Washington
Protestant Episcopal Church

THE LESSON OF HIS LIFE

WHEN ONE DISCUSSES BRIEFLY a man of such varied gifts as Thomas Jefferson, it is possible to touch no more than a small segment of his genius and his significance to our time. Statesman, author, educator, economist, architect, humanitarian: Jefferson ranks, with Benjamin Franklin, among the most versatile and intellectual men whom America has given to the world.

It has always seemed to me that the three things he asked to have inscribed on his tomb as accomplishments of his lifetime, ignored many of the contributions to his country which his own and future times consider of equal importance. It will be recalled that he wished to be remembered as "author of the Declaration of Independence; of the Statute for Religious Liberty in Virginia; and founder of the University of Virginia."

It was certainly made clear in Jefferson's historic controversy with Hamilton that he stood for the democratic ideal, as against the aristocratic; that, in his own time, he saw the basic issue between government and people. Of course Jefferson insisted that government should exist for the sake of the individual, to conserve the individual's liberties and freedom; rather than that the individual should exist to contribute to the greatness of an all-powerful state.

As one attempts thus briefly to summarize Jefferson's democratic philosophy, it might seem that a page is being taken from the history of our own generation, both in international and domestic affairs. It is easy to see with what passion Jefferson would have opposed the totalitarian theories of Nazism and Fascism; how he would have defended the democratic ideal against those who question the vitality and the eternal value of democracy.

But on the occasion of the second centennial of Jefferson's birth, it seems most important to me to remember that Jefferson would also have taken his place in the ranks of those who oppose present trends toward strengthening the autocratic powers of the federal government at the expense of state and local governments. This point seems to stand out so clearly in Jefferson's career and his writings, that it need only be stated to be established.

It cannot, by any means, be said that Jefferson was one of those who believe that government is a necessary evil. The fact that he was the author of the Declaration of Independence and played a leading role in the events leading up to and following the Revolution; that he served as the third President of the infant Republic, is sufficient evidence of his understanding that a strong and effective central government is necessary in a great nation. But he never ceased to insist that this government should be the servant, not the master, of its people.

Here to me is the lesson to be found in Jefferson's life for our years of emergency and transition. Whatever comes out of the present struggle, whatever steps may be undertaken to defend and preserve our nation during the war and the peace to follow, we shall find the safest guide to our conduct in this central theme of Jefferson's career.

His words furnish innumerable texts for those who oppose any tendency toward a dictatorial central government, at the expense of the basic liberties and freedoms of the common man, which Jefferson sought to preserve and protect throughout the whole of his long life.

—Frank E. Gannett

A VISION FOR THE WORLD

THOMAS JEFFERSON is as alive today as he was at the height of his career eight score years ago. In fire and blood his moral axioms are being tested and validated anew. Our generation is re-learning the hard way what his generation of Americans first learned through tears and blood that these United States came into being not for the purpose merely of adding another nationality to the world's complex of nations but for the purpose of witnessing and carrying a new vision of a human society based on human equality, human dignity and the right of every man to the freedom of conscience.

The tyranny against which Thomas Jefferson inveighed was mild in comparison with the Nazi-Fascist tyranny which has challenged our generation. If Jefferson were alive today he would see his vision for his United States become projected and magnified upon the larger canvas of the world's need.

Let us be sure, however, that while we project our vision upon the larger world scale we do not overlook the faults in our own immediate premises. As long as there are Negroes who still are denied the right to vote and the right to jobs, as long as there are Jews who are the victims of economic, social and political discrimination, as long as there are Chinese who are treated as an inferior race, Jefferson's vision is still unfulfilled in our own midst.

The difference between what we are and what he hoped we would become is the mandatory area of our future progress as a nation.

—ISRAEL GOLDSTEIN,
President of the Synagogue Council of America

FATHER OF DEMOCRACY

THOMAS JEFFERSON is more than a name to Americans and freedom loving people everywhere. His life and the philosophy which he evolved and handed down to us is a challenge to thinking people the world over. It is equally applicable to our lives as individuals and as a nation. That philosophy was in part tersely embodied in the preamble to our Declaration of Independence, of which Thomas Jefferson was the author, "that all men are created equal; that they are endowed by their Creator with certain inalienable rights; that among these are life, liberty, and the pursuit of happiness." We are further reminded in that memorable document that it is the function of the government to guarantee those rights—"a government whose powers are derived from the consent of the governed."

At this time in the history of the world when all nations are embroiled in a bitter conflict the words and counsel of Thomas Jefferson recur again and again. It is not debatable that if individuals and nations observed the right of all men to be free and to pursue happiness in their own way, there would be no occasion for war. Greed and lust for power and the acquisition of territory which belongs to others is the primary cause of war through history. It was their grim determination to resist tyranny and restore freedom to the world that precipitated the entrance of the United Nations into this titanic struggle.

Perhaps the most outstanding contribution which Thomas Jefferson made to us as a nation was the authorship of the Declaration of Independence which was based upon the firm determination of the Colonists to be free from control of a foreign nation. His passion for freedom—religious, economic and political —was further exemplified in the legislation which he drafted such as the bill he offered in the Virginia Legislature which was the first declaration for absolute religious liberty to be offered by a sovereign state in the history of the world.

Jefferson was a staunch advocate of higher educational opportunities for all the people that they might thus be enabled to reason their problems out to a logical conclusion. His personal library became the nucleus of our Library of Congress which is the most complete in the whole world. He was responsible for the University of Virginia and was active in its administration until his death. The University was built in sight of Jefferson's home.

Jefferson was a slaveholder himself, but his convictions were strong on the subject of freedom and he introduced a bill in the legislature of Virginia to abolish slavery. He was the father of our elective system and is known as the Father of Democracy. He founded the Republican Party in our American political life, now known as the Democratic Party. He believed in the ability of the people to rule themselves and that education was a prerequisite to the extension of self-government to all. Jefferson was firm in his belief in states rights lest the national government become tyrannical. Though he was a man of rare social accomplishments and fine taste, Jefferson despised pomp and ostentation and defied the social customs of the day in many ways. He was truly a man with the courage of his convictions, honest in his dealings with his fellow man, and made a contribution to our American way of life which has been equalled by few.

—WILLIAM GREEN,
President,
American Federation of Labor

JEFFERSON AND THE
BILL OF RIGHTS

THOMAS JEFFERSON, of course, did not originate the Bill of Rights. He had much to do with its amplification and in securing that it be embedded in the Constitution. His flaming insistence in the Declaration that men "are endowed by their Creator with certain inalienable rights" had much to do with implanting them in the fibre of American life.

Jefferson knew well the centuries of struggle in which men had died fighting bitterly for these rights. Step by step they had been secured through the Magna Charta, the growth of common law, the "Petition of Rights," and the Declaration of Rights, until they reached full flower in the new republic.

During the first century and a half of our national life we saw no serious challenge to the Bill of Rights. We extended them and we accepted them as the air we breathed. But for the last quarter of a century they have been incessantly attacked both from without and within our country.

In the hurricane of revolutions which have swept the world since the Great War, men, struggling with the wreckage and poverty of that great catastrophe and the complications of the machine age, have in despair surrendered their freedom for false promises of security and glory. Whether it be Fascism, Nazism, Communism, or their lesser followers, the result is the same. Every day they repudiate every principle of the Bill of Rights. And where they have triumphed the first security of men has been lost.

Theirs is a form of servitude, of slavery—a slipping back toward the Middle Ages. Whatever these ideologies are, they have one common denominator—the citizen has no inalienable rights. He is submerged into the State. Here is the most fundamental clash known to mankind—that is, free men and women, cooperating under orderly liberty, as contrasted with human beings made pawns of government; men who are slaves of despotism, as against free men who are the masters of the State.

Even in America, where liberty blazed brightest and by its glow shed light on all the others, liberty is not only besieged from without but it is challenged from within. Many, in honest belief, hold that we cannot longer accommodate the growth of science, technology and mechanical power to the Bill of Rights. But men's inventions cannot be of more value than men themselves. It would be better that we sacrifice something of economic efficiency than to surrender these primary liberties. In them lies a spiritual growth of men. Behind them is the conception which is the highest development of the Christian faith—the conception of individual freedom with brotherhood. From them is the fullest flowering of individual human personality.

Those who proclaim that the Machine Age created an irreconcilable conflict in which Liberty must be sacrificed should not forget the battles for these rights over the centuries, for let it be remembered that in the end these are undying principles which spring from the souls of men. We imagine conflict not because the principles of liberty are unworkable in a machine age, but because we have not worked them conscientiously or have forgotten their true meaning.

Neither would sacrifice of these rights add to economic efficiency nor would it gain in economic security, or find a single job or give a single assurance in old age. The dynamic forces which sustain economic security and progress in human comfort lie deep below the surface. They reach to those human impulses which are watered alone by freedom. The initiative of men, their enterprise, the inspiration of thought, flower in full only in the security of these rights.

And by practical experience under the Bill of Rights we have tested this truth. Down through a century and a half this American concept of human freedom has enriched the whole world. From the release of the spirit, the initiative, the cooperation, and the courage of men, which alone comes from these freedoms, has been builded this very machine age with all its additions of comfort, its reductions of sweat. Wherever in the world the system of individual liberty has been sustained, mankind has been better clothed, better fed, better housed, has had more leisure. Above all, men and women have had more self-respect. They have been more generous and of finer spirit. Those who scoff that liberty is of no consequence to the under-privileged and the unemployed, are grossly ignorant of the primary fact that it is through the creative and the productive impulses of free men that the redemption of those sufferers and their economic security must come. Any system which curtails these freedoms and stimulants to men destroys the possibility of the full production from which economic security alone can come.

Nor is respect for the Bill of Rights a fetter upon progress. It has been no dead hand that has carried the living principles of liberty over these centuries. Without violation of these principles and their safeguards we have amended the Constitution many times in the past century to meet the problems of growing civilization. We will no doubt do so many times again. New inventions and new ideas require the constant remolding of our civilization. The functions of government must be readjusted from time to time to restrain the strong and protect the weak. That is the preservation of liberty itself.

Jefferson was eternally right when he held that liberty comes only and lives only where the hard-won rights of men are held inalienable, where governments themselves may not infringe, where governments are indeed but the mechanisms to protect and sustain these principles. It was this concept for which America's sons have died on a hundred battlefields.

The purification of liberty from abuses, the restoration of confidence in the rights of men, from which come the release of the dynamic forces of advancing spirit and enterprise, are alone the methods through which the purpose of American life can be assured.

—HERBERT HOOVER

A UNIVERSAL FIGURE

THOMAS JEFFERSON was remarkable in many ways—for the variety of his interests, the unflagging vigor of his mind, and the freedom and utter tolerance of his spirit. But chiefly he was notable as one of the outstanding advocates and exemplars of democracy in the great age of democracy's advent in our civilization.

Jefferson was a democrat in a two-fold sense. Negatively, he suspected government as a necessary evil, to be watched for its acquisition and use of power against the common weal. Positively, he respected the people as the only true source of power, and sought always to protect and preserve their rights. Government was at its best but an agent of the people's will which must be free to make its own choices, try its own experiments, and seek its own desired ends. He was more proud of having been the author of the Virginia Bill of Rights than of having been a president of the United States, and was one of the few men in history who were uncorrupted by the allures of public office.

Jefferson's principles and practices seemed never so wise and beautiful as in this age when governments, conquering and subduing peoples in their own exercise of power, have reestablished tyranny and swept the world far back toward barbarism and a new dark age. Only through a new subjection of the state to the rights of men as in the Jeffersonian sense alone sacred and therefore supreme, can civilization be saved from ruin.

Thomas Jefferson ranks with George Washington, Benjamin Franklin and Abraham Lincoln as one of the four universal figures contributed by America to the pantheon of mankind. His name must ever be synonymous with that of Liberty, and thus immortal.

—JOHN HAYNES HOLMES,
Chairman, Board of Directors,
American Civil Liberties Union

SPIRITUAL ANCESTOR OF THE UNITED NATIONS

IN THE TWO CENTURIES that have elapsed since the birth of Thomas Jefferson, those rights of mankind which we deem to be self-evident and elementary have come more and more to be recognized and accepted; if progress at times has seemed slow or halting, the trend, as we look back, has been constant.

That there could come a period when the attempt would be made not only to destroy all that was so achieved but to turn back to world enslavement and to brutal conquest would be incredible if it had not happened. Yet such is the infamous design of our enemies which must be frustrated by their defeat.

It was Thomas Jefferson who wrote that among the inalienable rights with which men are endowed by their Creator are life, liberty, and the pursuit of happiness. It was he who framed a famous statute in which it was enacted that Almighty God created the mind free and that civil rights have no dependence on our religious opinions. Jefferson, among the founding Fathers, is the spiritual ancestor of the principles embodied in the Declaration of the United Nations that complete victory is essential to defend life, liberty, in-

60

dependence, and religious freedom in our own and other lands.

Within our heritage are the Declaration of Independence and the Bill of Rights; and we will not suffer them to be annulled.

—CORDELL HULL,
United States Secretary of State

A FIGHTING LIBERAL

WHEN I THINK of Thomas Jefferson I visualize a fighting liberal. To me he is not a mere "Founding Father," mummified in a wig and silk breeches, sacrosanct and untouchable. To me he is what I am sure he was to his contemporaries—a brave, warm-hearted, hard-hitting fighter for human rights and civil liberties. All of his life he fought for the things that he believed in, and he never compromised on principles. "Timid men," he once said, "prefer the calm of despotism to the boisterous sea of liberty." Jefferson was decidedly not one of those timid men.

What did Jefferson believe in? I think that Abraham Lincoln was right when he said that the principles of the author of the Declaration of Independence were the "axioms" of a free society. Among those principles were self-government, freedom, equality, justice, progress, the dignity of man, and the right to the pursuit of happiness—in short, democracy.

Consider, for instance, self-government. In Jefferson's day the upper classes and their spokesmen argued that men were too stupid and too depraved to be capable of governing themselves. Jefferson demolished this argument in two brief, devastating sentences.

"Sometimes it is said that man cannot be trusted with the government of himself. Can he, then, be trusted with the government of others?"

Occasionally one hears people say, 'Jefferson's ideas were good enough for a small, agricultural society, but they don't apply to a big, industrial country like modern America.' My reply is that his ideas are timeless and as eternal as human nature. So long as people anywhere strive to achieve a better life for their fellow men, Jefferson will remain a source of inspiration.

I am profoundly convinced that without a basic democratic ideology—that is, without the principles of Jefferson—it will be impossible for our world to secure a stable peace or to achieve economic security. We have seen enough horror in recent years to know that tyranny is the greatest evil that can afflict humanity. I hope that this generation has also learned the lesson that Jefferson knew and preached from the bottom of his heart—that freedom is the greatest good that man can possess.

Life without liberty is a brutish thing at the mercy of brutes. Without liberty there can be no science, no education, no peace, no decent relations between a man and his neighbor. Jefferson hammered at this lesson for half a century, saying it and writing it and living it and acting upon it. And when he got through, the American people had learned the lesson well.

John Adams' last words, "Thomas Jefferson still lives," were symbolic and prophetic. Jefferson lives and will always live. He had dedicated his whole life to the ideals of liberty and the pursuit of happiness, and today millions of men are fighting on a hundred battlefronts for those ideals. In the new age of peace and freedom that is emerging out of the present world tragedy, Jefferson will be honored by all progressive mankind as a major prophet.

—HAROLD L. ICKES,
United States Secretary of the Interior

AMERICAN TRADITION
AND OUTLOOK

MORE THAN ANY OTHER LEADER Thomas Jefferson is responsible both for the definiteness of our American social-political tradition and for its strength. Samuel Adams and Patrick Henry were earlier and more aggressive leaders for separation from Great Britain, George Mason was probably the deeper thinker in the new political philosophy, Benjamin Franklin was more successful in the management of both public and private affairs and was personally much better known abroad, George Washington was the wise and loved leader both in war and in peace, but Thomas Jefferson more than anyone else gave character and content to what we now recognize as the distinctive American tradition and outlook.

His actual wording of the Declaration of Independence gives it perennial power and influence. Its crisp phrases still ring: "We hold these truths to be self-evident," "laws of Nature and Nature's God," "a decent respect to the opinion of mankind," "all men are created equal," "certain unalienable rights," "life, liberty, and the pursuit of happiness," "governments . . . deriving their just powers from the consent of the governed," "are, and of right ought to be, free and independent states," "we mutually pledge our lives, our fortunes, and our sacred honor." As long as the spirit of freedom shall last, these words will stir men's souls.

Jefferson's abolition of entailed property and primogeniture in Virginia, spreading to the other states, destroyed legalized aristocracy. His Virginia statute for religious liberty, building on Roger Williams's earlier foundation in Rhode Island and supported later by Article VI of the Constitution and the first amendment, established, in time, the American doctrine of the separation of church and state.

By his fifty years of popular leadership in the cause of the common man he more than any other laid the foundation on which the Andrew Jackson period established the dominant American doctrine of manhood suffrage (although by certain "poll tax" laws it still fails of universality).

If he could have had his way slavery would have been peaceably abolished fifty years before the Civil War and state systems of public education including state universities would have been established fifty years earlier than they actually came.

As to the actual Bill of Rights now found in the Constitution, Jefferson would wish us to grant to George Mason the greater credit not simply for its formulation but for its actual inclusion in the Constitution. But as to the underlying tradition which now supports these rights in the American mind and conscience, that belongs most of all to Jefferson himself.

As today our people face a warring world, it is this social-political tradition of belief in the human individual—the definiteness and the strength of this tradition—which illumines and supports their effort both on the home front and at the battle front. It is their belief in the human rights which Jefferson so clearly defined that distinguishes our cause from that of our enemy. We fight that this cause may win now and forever.

—WILLIAM H. KILPATRICK,
*Professor Emeritus, Teachers College,
Columbia University*

CHAMPION OF THE COMMON MAN

THE PASSAGE OF THE YEARS has seen the figure of Thomas Jefferson loom ever larger in the minds of his countrymen. The partisan disputes which clouded the eyes of some of his contemporaries have faded away and he stands revealed as one of the truly great men our country has produced. More than that, his is a figure which looms high in the ranks of the immortal great of all nations in all time.

In an age of ever-increasing specialization, we look back with admiration at Jefferson's remarkable versatility. Political theorist, statesman, educator, architect, student of religion, paleontologist, farmer, lawyer and practical inventor—many subjects invited his curiosity. Nor was he a mere dilettante. To every field he brought a fresh inquiring mind: in each he left an imprint which pushed back the frontiers of human knowledge. Today even more than in Jefferson's time, we need men who can see beyond specialized fields into which human knowledge has become divided—men who can see life and society as a whole—who can relate each part to every other.

Jefferson's approach to life was not merely that of a scholar in his ivory tower. In an age when every one of us must actively struggle for freedom, we remember with gratitude that Jefferson devoted his whole life to this struggle. At home and abroad he battled for human freedom, and in so battling he played a tremendous part in establishing human freedom as one of the fundamental and lasting tenets of our Government.

Above all, in this age which has been so aptly called "The Century of the Common Man," we feel a special kinship with one who, perhaps more than any other of our early leaders, believed and trusted in the common man. Jefferson's whole life breathed a passionate belief in both the right and ability of the little man to determine his own destiny. Upon the two hundredth anniversary of his birth, we can do no better than to remember his comment on tyrants of another age. "The mass of humanity," he wrote, "has not been born with saddles on their backs nor a very few booted and spurred ready to ride them legitimately by the grace of God."

Today our enemies declare that they have been divinely equipped with boots and spurs to ride roughshod over the champions of freedom; but the spirit of Jefferson is still the spirit of the United Nations. It is our task to see to it that the spirit of Jefferson becomes the spirit of the entire world.

—FRANK KNOX,
United States Secretary of the Navy

THE GREAT OBJECTIVE

JEFFERSON EXPRESSED the liberal progressive idea of his day, "that the best government is the one that governs the least".

Today this great Jeffersonian principle is the stock argument of the hard shell tories and reactionaries by which they pick to establish the doctrine of laissez faire.

In Jefferson's day the common man's lot was made hard because the king and those who had his ear had charters that gave them monopolies in practically all the then known fields of business.

Jefferson by the above statement simply advocated the freeing of business from monopolistic control made possible by these charters. This Jeffersonian principle of government has really never been tried. It was not aimed at business in general but against these monopolies based on special privilege.

Today it is still a live issue. On the one side are those who favor big cartels and monopolies regulated and managed by the government in the interest of all the people. They believe the proper answer to protection of the individual is government control of the business, industrial, agricultural, and labor life of the nation. That really is Nazism.

On the other side are those who would use the power of government to achieve Jefferson's object—the destruction of special privilege through the enforcement of the anti-trust laws and similar legislation.

That great objective of Jefferson, the use of our national resources for the benefit of the people, is still to be attained. However the usefulness of his way of meeting it no longer remains because the structure has changed and become so complex that action by the government is the only way it can be met. But Jefferson's theory helped change the structure because through him the common man became articulate.

—ALF M. LANDON

FIGHTING FOR HIS PRINCIPLES

IT IS PARTICULARLY FITTING that the Bill of Rights Sesqui-Centennial Committee will this year sponsor the observance of the 200th anniversary of Thomas Jefferson's birth on April 13. Thomas Jefferson devoted his long and full life to the very principles for whose preservation we are now fighting a total war side by side with the other United Nations.

The American people have a proud heritage in the resources, the culture, the opportunities of their beloved country. Yet their deep love for this Democracy of ours springs mainly from other sources. It springs from an unshakable conviction in the justice of the political and social fundamentals which we, the American people, have established and demonstrated; the principle that government exists for men, not men for government; the principle of personal and economic liberty; the principle of racial and religious equality. The very safety of democracy depends upon the vigilant and active idealism of the American people.

This is even more true today than it was in Thomas Jefferson's day. The dangers which have beset our democratic way of life have intensified with the years. In recent years selfish and evil men—friends of a totalitarian system—have sought to undermine our people's government. Our people have come to realize that democracy can be safeguarded only by militant defense of the social and religious liberties guaranteed to all; by an awakened national spirituality and by the continual concern of a progressive people and their government for the social and economic well-being of all.

Democracy has proven and will continue to prove that it will keep the economic system going for the benefit and profit of business, labor and agriculture, without paying for this achievement in the sacrifice and destruction of the civil liberties and individual freedom which alone makes like worth living.

Thomas Jefferson and the men of his generation, who gave to posterity the precious document guaranteeing our civil liberties, would have cause to be proud of the Americans of today. Our people have made sacrifices. Unfortunately, they will have to make many more. But we are truly united in a determination to stamp out for all time the forces of tyranny. We are working shoulder to shoulder with the United Nations to secure and preserve our democratic way of life.

—HERBERT H. LEHMAN,
Director, Foreign Relief and
Rehabilitation Operations

ETERNALLY RIGHT

THE BEST WAY to honor the memory of Thomas Jefferson is to continue and complete his revolution. He believed and declared "that all men are created equal". That ideal was a hard saying in Jefferson's time; it is still hard.

To make democracy effective we must begin with fundamentals. Jefferson said that our inalienable rights have been bestowed by a Creator. Certain schoolmen have been telling us for more than half a century that the source of man's being was an ape, or an emoeba, or at best a butterfly, but certainly not God the Creator. This made us all just animals. Hitler carried this idea to its logical conclusion. If the people of Europe, including the Germans, are only animals they ought to be treated like animals. The schoolmen rejected Jefferson and Hitler refuted them by putting their unholy theories into practice. But the conscience of humanity recoils from this barbarism. Thinking men everywhere now recognize that both Hitler and the schoolmen are wrong; Jefferson is eternally right.

Human rights are inalienable because they are part of our nature. They were bestowed by the Creator and we all have them because we are all human; we can't lose them because we are sons of God. This means that if the white man has a natural right to political freedom, the colored man has it also. If the employer has a natural right to economic security the working man has it also. If our country has a right to international security all countries have it in equal measure.

What probability is there that we shall recognize universal human equality by making freedom and security effective here and abroad? What chance have we of continuing and completing Jefferson's revolution? Certainly, it were folly to fight for the ideals of democracy in Asia and Africa if we are not prepared to practice them at home.

At the present moment a large segment of our citizens do not believe in political equality. Hitler's absurdity of the master race was accepted here in the time of Jefferson. It is still with us. Millions of our people believe that somehow the white man is superior to the colored; as though God were concerned with pigmentation. The poll tax iniquity has never been rejected, even in national elections. It is a convenient device for keeping Negroes, Mexicans and poor whites in political slavery.

Nevertheless, the situation is not hopeless. Millions of citizens in the South sincerely believe in the philosophy of Thomas Jefferson and some day their voices will be heard. Then too, it seems probable that political leaders of the master race mentality are not being born any more, at least, not in such large numbers as heretofore; and this gives hope for the future.

With the federal government acting as mid-wife, economic security is being born in long and painful travail. The battle for industrial democracy is by no means won, but time, experience, education and a benevolent government have accomplished wonders. Reactionaries we still have in abundance but their ranks and their power are growing thinner.

By common consent, if not by default, the moral leadership of the nations has been bestowed on us. Ours is the high privilege of leading the way to a community of nations, a permanent court of international justice, sanctions against unjust aggressors and a program of reciprocal sacrifice for the common good. Our isolationists will try to stop us but God grant that we may rise nobly to meet this greatest challenge of our time. Thomas Jefferson would have it so.

—ROBERT E. LUCEY,
Archbishop of San Antonio, Texas

BUILDER OF HIS COUNTRY

"IT IS NECESSARY TO GIVE as well as take in a government like ours".

Thomas Jefferson, a builder of his country, was the author of those words.

Jefferson said other things, too—no less grand.

"I know of no safe depository of the ultimate powers of society", he said, "but the people themselves".

And, "There is a debt of service due from every man to his country, proportioned to the bounties which nature and fortune have measured on him".

Those are things which could have been said only by an American who conceived of his country as the kind of country which we want America *always* to be.

That is why we are fighting today. We have to fight to keep America that kind of place.

It is indeed necessary for each one of us to give of his best if we are to preserve the kind of America which Jefferson helped build.

—PAUL V. McNUTT,
Chairman, War Manpower Commission

FATHER OF THE BILL OF RIGHTS

IT IS MOST APPROPRIATE THAT THE Bill of Rights Sesqui-Centennial Committee has chosen this time to commemorate the political, philosophical, educational and human ideals and accomplishments of Thomas Jefferson, because he probably more than any statesman that ever lived, symbolized liberty, freedom, independence, culture in its broadest sense, the necessity of education for all, and last but not least, love and obedience to the Almighty who rules and guides the destinies of men and nations.

He was at once in himself one of America's greatest immortals and at the same time a great citizen of the rest of the world. What he thought and said and did although primarily for the consideration and benefit of his own country and his own people, was so universal in effect and application, that those very same accomplishments influenced greatly not only America but the rest of the civilized world.

Jefferson's acknowledged greatness, therefore, comes not altogether from the fact that he was constructively successful in an unlimited degree as a Statesman, Minister Plenipotentiary, Secretary of State, Vice-President and President, and because an incomparable administrator and executive in every capacity in which he served so unselfishly, but his real immortality comes chiefly from his all around intellectuality and spirituality and humanity which permitted him to create a philosophy of life serviceable for human beings all over.

In spite of his mighty accomplishments in so many spheres of life's activity, he was a most modest individual and notwithstanding his aristocratic birth and his high social position, he believed intensely in the common people and felt and taught always that to all, regardless of race, color, creed, equal liberty to think and to act and to worship should be afforded at all times, and that there should never be any discriminations of any kind based upon such adventitious circumstances as race, creed or color.

It is typical of him also that the political offices he held are not mentioned in the epitaph he wrote for his tombstone. He wished to be remembered as the "Author of the Declaration of Independence, the Statute of Virginia for Religious Liberty, and Father of the University of Virginia".

He always believed and taught that all power is derived from the people and that peace and tranquility throughout the land could be best secured by a strong Constitution conceived in the thought that by these means all the blessings of liberty could be best obtained for ourselves and transmitted to posterity. He always most vigorously advocated under all circumstances the rights of the individual citizen and of the individual states, and he believed that the Constitution should be of a character flexible enough to permit amendments from time to time as conditions changed, so that always there would be guaranteed to all citizens their natural and inalienable rights.

Jefferson, therefore, may very properly be considered by reason of his contributions in thought and action and because of the things he advocated and for which he fought, the spiritual father of the Bill of Rights, and we know he is today in spirit with all good Americans and other courageous hearts who are fighting in different parts of the world to maintain and preserve the Jeffersonian ideals and principles so well embodied in the Declaration of Independence, the Constitution of the United States and the Bill of Rights, documents that will, until time is no more, aid in perpetuating America as the home of the free and the brave, and the land to which the oppressed of all nations may always look for encouragement and help.

—JEREMIAH T. MAHONEY

THE GOOD SPIRIT OF AMERICA

FOR US EUROPEAN INTELLECTUALS the transplantation to these shores was a great experience, a great relief for which we cannot be grateful enough. From deranged, poisoned narrowness we came into the largeness, into the expansive atmosphere of a country of happy origins, happy premises, happy history, where, contrary to the over-experienced, tired and somber Europe, life is determined by confidence, hope and a hearty faith in humanity and the human progress toward the better. Despite all antagonisms and differences of conviction which naturally divide even this country into competing camps, the clean, benevolent and spiritually sound principles and the moral code of conduct upon which the Union was originally established by the founding fathers, is still alive and decisive here; they form the myth of this two hundred year old community, the national tradition. There is a straight line running from Thomas Jefferson, the author of the immortal document called the Declaration of Independence, to Henry A. Wallace who on May 8th, 1942 delivered his famous speech about the Century of the Common Man, the speech entitled "The Price of Free World Victory". If we ask ourselves, however, what is the conserving and all-pervading characteristic element of America's political philosophy, the answer is: it is the principle that "men are endowed by their Creator with certain inalienable rights" and that among those inalienable rights is "the pursuit of happiness".

Happiness as a natural right of man—that is a strangely daring and naïve thought which could never have found its way into a state document in the old Europe; it belongs to the optimistic pioneer spirit of America. Schopenhauer, a German philosopher, has called optimism "ruthless" and declared all life to be essentially suffering, and that to speak to man about happiness was to deride him. But the American thought of the claim to happiness does not contradict the suffering innate in all earthly life; it does not deny, unpiously, the religious urge for salvation of man. What it denies is rather the by no means God-sent, by no means inevitable suffering, but the suffering caused by man's own laziness and folly, the suffering that is an insult to human reason and honor, and whose intelligent abolition is the duty before God as well as before man. At the basis of the American idea of human right to happiness is the distinction between inevitable and definitely evitable, indeed scandalous suffering; it is an idea inspired by faith in social progress, in the duty to better the conditions of life on earth; and for this idea America fights in this war too.

The Four Freedoms of the Atlantic Charter are nothing but a new expression of the human right to happiness; they are a joyous social message which America in the name of the United Nations opposes to the evil and disbelieving sinister plan of World enslavement harbored by the Axis powers: the price of Free World Victory. In all the misery that this earth-embracing war, this civil war of humanity, brings with it, we must not forget that it also holds great hopes, great possibilities for a joyous future, a better, more reasonable community life and cooperation of the peoples, for the enhancement of human happiness. This struggle, this victory of freedom in which we trust, and the peace to be shaped afterwards gives a great chance to humanity to reach a new level of social maturity and majority, and to close many sources of unnecessary and therefore disgraceful suffering. The good spirit of America which counts the pursuit of happiness among the inalienable rights of man may be our guarantee that this great chance will not be passed by.

—THOMAS MANN

OUR INSPIRATION

NOW THAT THE SHADOW OF THE AXIS slowly commences its retreat from the face of the earth, it is appropriate that we should look for a vigorous reaffirmation of the principles of democratic government. It is fitting that we should look to Thomas Jefferson for our inspiration. As Washington is revered as the Father of our Country, Jefferson will always be remembered as the Father of the Rights of Man.

Democratic government, not geared for warfare, takes time to mobilize our industrial plant and equipment so that implements of destruction may be turned out, so also we must change our thinking. After a little more than a year of conflict we are just beginning to understand the meaning of "total war." Men and women who have not yet become part of that "totality" will be mobilized during the coming months. More and more acutely we are beginning to realize that total participation is necessary for a democratic government to survive. This is true in times of peace as well as in times of war. Our way of live is secure in proportion to the acceptance of responsibility by the people who live under American institutions and pay lip service to them.

Jefferson recognized that the limited concept of citizenship must be expanded; that unless everyone, regardless of race or degree of wealth, has an opportunity to participate, those guarantees of human freedom and human dignity written into our Constitution would fail. He was the first great proponent of a philosophy of government peculiar to American life, which has remained firm in all America's growth and evolution. This philosophy has culminated during the administration of President Roosevelt. This is the point of view that it is necessary to lift averages and to spread opportunities. Over a period of a century and a half we have been establishing minimum standards of public education, public recreation, public health, working conditions and public assistance for those who are temporarily deprived of opportunity due to conditions outside their control.

Jefferson fought the early battles to make this concept live and from that day to this the movement has been steadily forward and upward. This philosophy has drawn millions of oppressed peoples to our land. It has given hope to those weary of the hatreds of the Old World. It still lives today because it inspired confidence in man's continued desire to be free and in return for his freedom to give back something. That is why we fix minimum standards because without certain minimum requirements men and women cannot fit themselves to assume the responsibility of citizenship.

In his day another dictator was marching across

Europe, extinguishing liberty wherever he found it. Most of the statesmen of Europe adopted a cynical pessimism which affected even some of our statesmen in the New World. But Jefferson became the articulate embodiment in the average man's instinct for improvement when opportunity was given him.

Jefferson assumed no leadership, but rather he was forced into a position of leadership by circumstances. His leadership was in response to a call from millions of Americans who had been inarticulate. In history he stands out in our minds as the embodiment of America's better self. He voiced the young surge of confidence and idealism which is at the heart of our nation. To study his life and the years when he gave our new nation direction, will provide for us, year in and year out, in war or in peace, the desire, the energy and the will to grow, not at the cost of the individual but due to his growth. His philosophy gives us an undying faith "in a government founded not on the fears and follies of man but on his reason and the predominance of his social over his dissocial passions."

—NEWBOLD MORRIS,
President of the Council of the City of New York

A REVOLUTIONARY SPIRIT

TWO HUNDRED YEARS AGO there was born in Albemarle County, in western Virginia, a child destined to become one of America's greatest leaders. No other statesman of our early days had so strong an influence on the shaping of American democracy, both for his own time and for the generations to follow, as did Thomas Jefferson.

His basic faith and philosophy are nowhere better expressed than in the preamble to Jefferson's most famous piece of writing—the Declaration of Independence. All men, it proclaimed to the world, are created equal, and they are endowed by their Creator with certain rights, among which are Life, Liberty and the Pursuit of Happiness.

To build a nation on such a credo was revolutionary indeed, and Jefferson gave the rest of his life to the service of his country and his state, trying to put his principles into active practice. In the Virginia legislature he worked sucessfully for legal reforms and the improvement of the penal code. Himself a gifted scholar, linguist, architect and philosopher, he was a staunch advocate of free and liberalized education, of a disestablished church in the new United States, and of the abolition of slavery.

Yet it is not for his political acts and his administration of the highest office in the nation that Jefferson is most to be remembered and honored today. It is for his amazingly democratic and far-seeing attitude of mind—an attitude which America greatly needs in these troubled years. At a time when the large majority of the European population was illiterate, oppressed, and despised by its rulers, Thomas Jefferson dared to declare his belief that man was endowed by nature with reason and an innate sense of justice; "that he could be restrained from wrong and protected in right by moderate powers confided to persons of his own choice and held to their duties by dependence on his own will". Seasoned with Locke's philosophy, and in the face of Federalist scorn of the people's ability to rule, Jefferson contended that men accustomed to thinking and reasoning for themselves could be more easily and safely governed than those debased by ignorance and oppression. "I have sworn upon the altar of God," he wrote in 1800, "eternal hostility against every form of tyranny over the mind of man."

These words of a great American who lived two centuries ago cannot be uttered too often today. Throughout most of Europe and much of Asia the forces of evil and darkness are exercising their tyranny over the minds and the bodies of men. Against those forces we of the United Nations must wage relentless war in the revolutionary spirit of Thomas Jefferson until men and women everywhere are free in mind, body and spirit.

—PHILIP MURRAY,
    President,
    Congress of Industrial Organizations

FOR FUTURE WORLD WELFARE

IT IS WELL TO OBSERVE the 200th anniversary of Thomas Jefferson's birth. He was one of the greatest Americans, and it might be well on this occasion to recall that he was not, as some present-day commentators declare, either an isolationist or an Anglophobe. He was too wise and too practical a statesman to be either. When writing to President Monroe concerning the announcement of the Monroe Doctrine, he said:

"The question presented by the letters you have sent me is the most momentous which has ever been offered to my contemplation since that of independence. That made us a nation; this sets our compass and points the course which we are to steer through the ocean of time opening on us. . . .

"One nation, most of all, could disturb us in this pursuit; she now offers to lead, aid and accompany us in it. By acceding to her proposition, we detach her from the bands, bring her mighty weight into the scale of free government, and emancipate a continent at one stroke which might otherwise linger long in doubt and difficulty. Great Britain is the one nation which can do us the most harm of any one, or all on earth; and with her on our side we need not fear the whole world. With her, then, we should most sedulously cherish a cordial friendship, and nothing would tend more to knit our affections than to be fighting once more, side by side, in the same cause."

On another occasion he wrote to Robert R. Livingston in Paris as follows:

"The day that France takes possession of New Orleans, we must marry ourselves to the British fleet and nation. We must turn all our attention to a maritime force . . . and, having formed and connected together with a Power which may render reinforcements of her settlements here impossible to France, make the first cannon which shall be fired in Europe be signal for the tearing up of any settlement she may have made, and for holding the two continents of America in sequestration for the common purposes of the United British and American nations."

These statements indicate clearly that, were Jefferson living today, he would be in wholehearted accord with what most unprejudiced statesmen realize, namely, that the continued union of Great Britain and ourselves is essential not only to victory but to the future welfare of the world.

—G. ASHTON OLDHAM,
Bishop of Albany
Protestant Episcopal Church

THOMAS JEFFERSON: A PORTRAIT

By Saul K. Padover

JAMES RUSSELL LOWELL said that Thomas Jefferson was the "first American man" and the best thinker of his day. Abraham Lincoln considered his principles the "definitions and axioms of a free society". Woodrow Wilson thought him immortal because of his attitude toward mankind. The world at large has always regarded him as the embodiment of American democratic idealism. Nevertheless, he is not as intimately known as he should be. A curious quality of elusiveness hovers over the reputation of Thomas Jefferson.

One of the reasons for this elusiveness is the subtlety of his mind and the complexity of his character. The most wide-ranging intellect of his day, he was at the same time the champion of democratic rights. A gentleman of wealth and position, he became the revered leader of the comon people. The most successful political figure of his generation, he never made a political speech. A party leader of matchless adroitness, he had practically no personal contact with his followers. As a political leader, he was oblique and indirect, a master of the flanking movement. A wily strategist, he outmaneouvered his opponents and left them floundering in angry helplessness. He was supple but firm, soft-spoken but uncompromising, and his enemies, used to the bluntnes of a John Adams or an Alexander Hamilton, could not quite understand him. They thought he was Machiavelli.

But he was as American as his background, and that was quite American. He was born, 200 years ago, on the frontier in western Virginia, on land which his father had personally cleared, in a region where there were practically no white settlers. The Jefferson homestead was set in the midst of dense forests.

Jefferson was thus a frontiersman, and not a mansion-bred aristocrat (though his mother came from an eminent family), as is commonly supposed. The frontier, where he spent his childhood and youth, had a basic influence upon his mind and character. It taught him the virtues of self-reliance, common sense, and, above all, a deep respect for the other fellow. The frontier, in other words, helped to mould him into an American democrat.

But there were other influences in his development. Foremost among them was his father, Colonel Peter Jefferson. Colonel Jefferson was an early American pioneer of the classic type, one of those rugged and hard-muscled men whose strength and courage broke the wilderness and opened it up to civilization. He was, it is important to keep in mind, of modest birth, self-made and self-educated. A giant in stature, Colonel Peter was respected far and wide for his sterling qualities. Even the Indians, who had no reason to love white men, admired Colonel Jefferson and often stopped at his house.

Colonel Jefferson died when Thomas was a boy of fourteen, leaving him heir to a considerable property, an estate of about 1,400 acres and a fine name that was more precious than gold. From his father Thomas had learned the arts of the pioneer—to ride, to shoot, to paddle a canoe—and the craft of the woodsman and farmer. From him also he had learned respect for truth and love of knowledge, as well as severe intellectual discipline and physical endurance.

Thomas Jefferson, like his father, was a strong and healthy man. In the course of a long life he rarely had a serious illness, and when he died, in his eighty-fourth year, all his teeth were in his mouth and were all sound.

The first thing that struck people about Jefferson was his size; the second, his carrot-red hair. Six feet two and a half inches in height, he was taller than his colleague George Washington, but not quite as massive. Thin and muscular, somewhat gangly and long-legged, he was a little awkward in his movements. His complexion was ruddy, weather-beaten, the skin of a man who spent hours daily outdoors, on horseback. Nobody ever thought him handsome, except in conversation, when his hazel eyes would light up and glow with animation.

He had deep reserves of moral strength and knowledge, and these gave him that poise and confidence which nothing, short of personal bereavement, could ever shake. Women found him charming and men were atracted to him by a quiet force of personality that was never aggressive or assertive. He exerted influence almost effortlessly, simply by being himself. There was something about him, some inner light, that set him apart as a leader of men. He was impressive, even when he wore old slippers.

Warm-hearted and affectionate, devoted to his family and to his friends, he loved nature and all things that were capable of growth. Cruelty and violence filled him with abhorrence. A man like Napoleon Bonaparte, the Hitler of his day, revolted him. He looked upon the conqueror of Europe as a "maniac" and a "bandit", as the "very worst of all human beings . . . having inflicted more misery on mankind than any other who had ever lived".

He thus described Napoleon:

"The Attila of the age . . . the ruthless destroyer of ten millions of the human race, whose thirst for blood appeared unquenchable, the great oppressor of the rights and liberties of the world . . . In civil life a cold-blooded, calculating, unprincipled usurper, without a virtue".

In contrast to the war-waging dictator of Europe, Jefferson was able to point to his own record as Chief Executive. He had the unique distinction of doubling the territory of his country, by purchase of the Louisiana Territory and not by conquest. The eight years of his Presidency were marred by no violence and no bloodshed. In his old age he told a friend: "I have the consolation to reflect that during the period of my administration not a drop of the blood of a single fellow citizen was shed by the sword of war or of the law".

Probably no other country than America could have produced Jefferson. Certainly no other country ever produced his like—a philosopher, a scientist, a statesman, a tribune of the common people, a leader who formulated the basic ideals by which his nation lives.

Like Sir Francis Bacon two centuries earlier, Jefferson made all knowledge his province. His intellectual and scientific interests are astounding. He was a violinist, a surveyor, a botanist, an ethnologist, a geologist, an astronomer, a mathematician, an agronomist, a horticulturist, and a general inventor. To many of these sciences he made genuine contributions. A glance through his letters shows that he discussed such subjects as rice, foundries, Greek and Latin languages, agriculture, thermometers, physical instruments, gardening, gunnery, fortifications, poisons, medicine, weaving, weights and measures, musical instruments, education, distillation of sea water, Indian languages, religion, silk culture, spinning machines, sulphur, olive trees, silver mines, tides, viticulture, speedometers, saw mills, sheep, meteoric stones, plows, coinage (he organized the dollar-unit which is still the basis of our currency system), steam power, canals, chemistry, almanacs, and torpedoes. He knew something about everything, and about some things he knew a great deal.

But over and above all this Jefferson stands out by reason of his great vision, a vision that is tied to the hopes and aspirations of common people the world over. His life was dedicated to the ideal of freedom.

The Declaration of Independence is Jefferson's monument and the quintessence of his idealism, which is, at the same time, America's idealism. Into the Declaration he poured his soul and his moral fervor. The magnificent phrases of the document burn with hatred of injustice and faith in mankind.

Underlying the Jeffersonian philosophy is the idea of the inherent goodness of men. Jefferson knew that without such a belief, democracy was an impossibility and self-government a travesty. Goodness meant also mutual respect and impartial justice. To Jefferson the dignity of any individual, regardless of origin or status, was sacred. Mutual respect was the base for any worthwhile civlization. Without it, there could be neither liberty nor the pursuit of happiness.

He had faith in progress and in man's capacity to learn and to improve himself. Of progress he said: "I expect it to be made here, under our democratic stimulants, on a great scale, until every man is potentially an athlete in body and an Aristotle in mind." He believed that men were able to appreciate the truth if the truth was presented to them fairly and honestly. Consequently he fought for a free press, which he considered more important than government itself. "Were it left to me to decide whether we should have a government without newspapers, or newspapers without a government, I should not hesitate a moment to prefer the latter." He believed that liberty "cannot be guarded but by the freedom of the press", and he defended the newspapers even when he was the victim

96

of unfair attacks. "Within the pale of truth", he said, "the press is a noble institution, equally the friend of science and of civil liberty."

To a friend he remarked: "We have spent the prime of our lives in procuring them (the young men of America) the precious blessings of liberty. Let them spend theirs in showing that it is the great parent of science and virtue; and that a nation will be great in proportion as it is free." On another occasion he said: "The cultivation of science is an act of religious duty." He knew that nothing was more fatal to freedom and human dignity than ignorance. The prerequisite of freedom was knowledge.

But knowledge and learning were not sufficient if confined to a select few. To Jefferson it was axiomatic that only on a foundation of popular education could freedom be secured. As he told Colonel Yancey in 1816: "If a nation expects to be ignorant and free, in a state of civilization, it expects what never was and never will be."

He devoted years of his life to the advancement of public education. His bills "for the more general diffusion of knowledge" among the people, which he introduced in the Virginia legislature, entitle him to be considered the father of America's free public school system. On the subject of the diffusion of knowledge, he wrote to his friend George Wythe, the great Virginia jurist:

"No other sure foundation can be devised, for the preservation of freedom and happiness . . . Preach, my dear Sir, a crusade against ignorance; establish and improve the law for educating the common people . . . the tax which will be paid for this purpose is not more than the thousandth part of what will be paid to kings, priests and nobles, who will rise up among us if we leave the people in ignorance."

Throughout history, Jefferson knew, men had always been tricked, confused, and then enslaved, principally because they were deprived of knowledge. He was, therefore, determined that this should never happen in America. Here he envisioned a democratic state founded on mass education aiming to achieve the happiness that comes from enlightenment.

"The brier and the bramble," he wrote, "can never become the vine and olive, but their asperities may be softened by culture, and their properties improved to usefulness. . . In the present spirit of extending to the great mass of mankind the blessings of instruction, I see a prospect of great advancement of the human race."

Freedom and happiness—to Jefferson these words were almost interchangeable—could be achieved only by enlightened citizens and maintained by alert ones. For Jefferson was afraid of the potential power of government. In Europe governments were almost invariably oppressive, brutal, and ignorant. No major people in Jefferson's day had succeeded in putting a bridle upon its insatiable rulers for any length of time, and he was frankly distrustful of the governmental leviathan. He knew that all government was, in essence, a monopoly—a monopoly of power over the lives and consciences of the citizens—and he was convinced that it must be watched with a perpetually suspicious eye. "Experience hath shewn, that even under the best forms, those entrusted with power have, in time, and by slow operations, perverted it into tyranny." He urged, therefore, that government should be fenced in by strictly limited constitutional powers and kept in bounds—that is, prevented from infringing upon the liberties and happiness of the citizens—by a wide distribution of the suffrage.

"Every government," he wrote, "degenerates when trusted to the rulers of the people alone. The people themselves therefore are its only safe depositories. And to render them safe, their minds must be improved to a certain degree . . . The influence over government must be shared by all the people. If every individual . . . participates of the ultimate authority, the government will be safe".

Today, two hundred years after he was born, Jefferson looms greater than ever. The centuries have added to his moral stature and his appeal transcends national boundaries. The child of the American frontier has emerged as one of the towering figures of history, a teacher of mankind who voiced its undying aspirations.

To lovers of liberty, Jefferson is timeless in his inspiration. Today, in particular, hundreds of millions of people throughout the world can appreciate his belief that freedom is "the most sacred cause that ever man was engaged in". Without the "precious blessing" of freedom, he felt, life had neither sense nor dignity. He had faith in mankind and he was convinced that some day freedom would be won by all men. The struggle would be titanic—"rivers of blood must yet flow, and years of desolation pass over; yet the object is worth rivers of blood, and years of desolation."

PIONEER OF INDEPENDENCE

THOMAS JEFFERSON, had he been alive in our time, would have been among the first to sense the threat to liberty, and to human cooperation inherent in his philosophy, which our armies and our people are opposing today.

He lived for the freedoms he set forth as the author of our Declaration of Independence. Thomas Jefferson was a pioneer in the cause of political independence and the rights of mankind and today his spirit is expressed daily by the millions of Americans in action.

The cause of the United Nations is symbolic of the tolerance and democracy which Jefferson preached and which we as a people are determined shall forever endure.

—FRANCES PERKINS,
United States Secretary of Labor

A BOLD FAITH

THE HERITAGE which Thomas Jefferson bequeathed to his fellow Americans is the gift of his faith in them.

It was a bold faith. The new republic which he had helped to create lacked many of the elements that might insure a union. It had no unity of blood or philosophy or religion. Its tradition, if any were ever to bind it, was yet to be formed. It held no guaranty of precedent. Its claim to nationhood rested on the unproved theory that all who possess the will to freedom are one people.

It would have been easy to pick a course of careful cynicism, to design a government for the people but neither of them nor by them. Jefferson chose instead the reality of self-government.

The years that have intervened have fulfilled his trust. The nation has grown in strength and unity beyond the dream of Jefferson. What had been bold theory has become an established fact. The faith of a man in us has been tested time and again, and the country is now meeting the supreme test.

The faith of Jefferson in us has become our faith in ourselves.

—JAMES P. POPE,
Director, Tennessee Valley Authority

SYMBOL OF THE FREE MAN

WITH THE WORLD TORN by a global war precipitated by the totalitarian Axis powers, it is timely to look in retrospect upon the life work and ideals of Thomas Jefferson, the classic spokesman of the democratic tradition in the Americas.

Thomas Jefferson was the exponent of a philosophy which emphasizes the importance of the individual, insisting that the state was the agent of the individual and not his master. To him the personality of the individual should be given the widest opportunity for development and full expression. This is only possible under the democratic system in which freedom of speech, freedom of the press, freedom of assembly, the right of petition, the right of trial by jury, habeas corpus, and freedom of worship are not only allowed but are considered an inevitable condition to the existence of free men.

Under the totalitarian state, there are no four freedoms and the state is glorified as the supreme end to which the individual must give absolute obedience and loyalty. In the Axis countries including Germany, Italy and Japan, the individual is sacrificed for the good of the state and has no rights that the state is bound to respect.

Thomas Jefferson is a symbol of the free man which is a complete negation of the totalitarian ideal which looks upon man as an incident and a means to an end, namely the consolidation of state power for aggression and world dominion. Labor, all minority groups and lovers of liberty cannot be too diligent in giving expression to the Jeffersonian conception of democracy.

—A. PHILIP RANDOLPH,
President, Brotherhood of
Sleeping Car Porters

JEFFERSON'S CREED

EQUAL AND EXACT JUSTICE to all men, of whatever state or persuasion, religious or political; peace, commerce, and honest friendship with all nations—

A jealous care of the right of election by the people—

Absolute acquiescence in the decisions of the majority, the vital principle of republics, from which there is no appeal but to force, the vital principle and immediate parent of despotism—

The supremacy of the civil over the military authority; economy in the public expense, that labor may be lightly burdened; the honest payment of our debts and sacred preservation of the public faith; encouragement of agriculture, and of commerce as its handmaid; the diffusion of information and the arraignment of all abuses at the bar of public reason; freedom of religion; freedom of the press; freedom of person under the protection of the habeas corpus; and trial by juries impartially selected—

—SAM RAYBURN,
*Speaker of the
House of Representatives*

ACROSS THE YEARS

THE POSITION OF THOMAS JEFFERSON in American history is fixed beyond the powers of words to illumine or define.

As one of those whose vision and wisdom fashioned the structure of the Republic and as the third President chosen to direct its destinies, Thomas Jefferson has his place amongst the immortals.

The measure of his influence upon American thought is less easy to determine for new events as they occur and new crises as they arise call forth a deepened sense of his greatness.

As architect and builder, Thomas Jefferson knew balance and symmetry and beauty. He understood the elements not only of sound construction but also of classic grace of design. The new Republic on whose structure he labored was planned similarly both with soundness and with the beauty of perfect balance.

Jefferson loved nature as few of our national leaders have loved it. The tilling of fields and the garnering in of harvests he knew well and he found them good. His faith in man was as fundamental as his faith in the orderly processes of nature.

Democracy was to Jefferson a recognition of the dignity of human spirit and he gave unremitting effort to its defense. He recognized that the struggle to uphold democracy must continue as long as there are foes who threaten it. His faith in its survival and advance was unwavering.

The words of his letter to John Adams in 1821 speak eloquently across the years to the troubled hearts of his countrymen today.

"I shall not die without a hope that light and liberty are on a steady advance. We have seen indeed once within the record of history, the complete eclipse of the human mind continuing for centuries . . . even should the cloud of barbarism and despotism again obscure the liberties of Europe, this country remains to preserve and restore light and liberty to them. In short the flames kindled on the 4th of July, 1776, have spread over too much of the globe to be extinguished by the feeble engines of despotism; on the contrary, they will consume these engines and all who work them."

—RUTH BRYAN OWEN ROHDE,
*Former United States Minister
to Denmark*

ABOVE MATERIAL THINGS

IT IS FITTING that in celebrating the 200th anniversary of Thomas Jefferson's birth we should re-examine the Bill of Rights, for it perhaps epitomizes his whole philosophy better than anything else which he had the major part in writing.

We are at present engaged in a world conflict against a conception of government and of life which lowers the respect for human personality. If people are to be robots, doing the bidding of one man, we can not look upon them with the same interest which we would feel in free men engaged in developing themselves to live in a world where their opinions and actions would shape their civilization.

Thomas Jefferson had great confidence in the possibility of the development of the common man. That is why he fought for education. That is why his concept of government gave increasing responsibility to the individual; because he knew that responsibility would bring growth. Today when we see barbarism and cruelty grow in those countries where responsibility has been removed from the individual and invested in a few people who constitute themselves a government which can not be questioned by the ordinary citizen, we realize more than ever before that Jefferson's concept, epitomized in the Bill of Rights, must be brought home to each and every one of us. If we hope to preserve the Democracies of the world and make them responsive to the will of the people, and instruments for providing these inalienable rights of life, liberty, and the pursuit of happiness, which to Jefferson were the objectives for which government was set up, then we must have responsible citizens. Every child in a democracy who is to learn to develop himself into a true citizen of his own nation, should not only study the life of Jefferson, but his philosophy, which set the things of the mind and of the heart above material things and made material things serve the ends which the mind and heart conceived.

—ELEANOR ROOSEVELT

THE DOCTRINE OF
NATURAL RIGHTS

OF ALL THE ELEMENTS embraced in the precious legacy
which Thomas Jefferson bequeathed to his countrymen, the greatest and most beneficent is the following
clause: "that all men are created equal, that they are
endowed by their Creator with certain inalienable
rights." To be sure, Jefferson did not invent the doctrines of human equality and natural rights. They are
rooted in the teaching of Christ, and they were dimly
grasped by some of the ancient pagans, e.g. Cicero and
the Stoics. The great importance of Jefferson's reaffirmation is its expression in one brief and striking sen-
tence in a document which is venerated by Americans
equally with the Constitution.

These fundamental truths are particularly in need
of emphasis today, for two reasons: First, because they
are denied by the great totalitarian powers; second, because they have for some time been rejected or ignored
by large groups in our own academic circles. Very few
Americans defend or approve the doctrines of race
superiority and subjection of the individual to the
State, as proclaimed and practiced by Nazism. Never-

theless, a majority, probably, of the teachers of the social sciences in our secular colleges and universities would, if they were logical, accept the second of these abominable doctrines. For they deny the existence of natural rights, and the sacredness of human personality. In their view, the human individual has no inherent, congenital rights nor any such thing as intrinsic worth. All his rights and worth are derived from the State or from Society. Men who accept this doctrine can denounce the philosophy of Nazism only at the cost of intellectual self stultification. The repition and the proclamation, in season and out of season, of Jefferson's immortal assertion of human equality and natural rights should prove very helpful in counteracting the effects of the false teaching of our pedagogical authorities. Finally, it should be noted that the author of the Declaration of Independence places natural rights upon a logical and metaphysical basis—their only adequate foundation—namely, the Creative act of God.

—MONSIGNOR JOHN A. RYAN,
*Director, Department of Social Action,
National Catholic Welfare Conference*

FREEDOM'S STRONGEST WEAPON

THIS YEAR OUR NATION CELEBRATES the 200th anniversary of a man whose contributions to the liberty of mankind seems just as new and just as needed today as they were at the height of his career. The whole world places its hope in the vision of Thomas Jefferson. His passion for freedom, perpetuated in our democratic form of government, is the strongest safeguard we have today, and the guiding star of struggling peoples everywhere who have lost individuality and identity under the totalitarian rule of dictators.

Jefferson desired that, after his death, he should be remembered, not as having ruled the American people, not as vice-president, or secretary of state, not as minister to France, or as a supreme party leader, but as the author of the Declaration of Independence, and of the Virginia Statute of Religious Freedom, and as the Father of the University of Virginia. Freedom of the intellect from dictation, superstition, and ignorance he recognized as the strongest weapon in any struggle against oppression or bigotry.

The doctrine which Jefferson penned virtually word for word with his own hand and which rightfully won for him the title of the greatest political philosopher of the 18th century was startlingly new then for Europe—and apparently still is unfamiliar to many of its countries today, where drudgery for the happiness of others is the watchword. How different is the conception of individual rights enunciated by Jefferson in the Declaration of Independence: "We hold these truths to be self-evident—that all men are created equal; that they are endowed by their Creator with certain unalienable rights; that among these are life, liberty and the pursuit of happiness."

It is hard to realize how revolutionary Jefferson's second major accomplishment appeared in those days. His draft of a law for religious freedom in Virginia, initiating the separation of church and state, was interpreted in many quarters as an attack on Christianity. When it appeared that he would be elected to the presidency, many New England women actually buried their Bibles or hid them in mattresses. Yet the spirit of tolerance which he did so much to foster is the guarantee that bigotry can never gain a foothold in the public affairs of this nation—a guarantee which is preserved forever in our Bill of Rights.

That ignorance breeds autocracy was the philosophy which prompted him in his third great work: creation of the University of Virginia, to give scope to the illimitable freedom of the human mind. His motto for the University of Virginia can still be our guide today:

> "Ye shall know the truth, and the
> truth shall make you free."

—LEVERETT SALTONSTALL,
Governor of Massachusetts

A PRACTICAL IDEALIST

JEFFERSON, MORE THAN ANY OTHER American states-man, realized the full implications of a belief in human equality and freedom. He was not merely an idealist willing to state his convictions as truths requiring no proof from history or science; he was also a practical statesman incessantly pursuing the realization of his ideals. He was no more bound by the interests of his class than by the dogmas of his philosophy. A large land-owner, he urged the broadening of the electorate to include small owners. A slave owner, leading a party generally dominated by slave owners, he urged steps toward early emancipation. He secured the disestablishment of the church to which he himself belonged.

The breadth and the practical sense of Jefferson's political approach to problems makes him peculiarly susceptible to misunderstanding by narrower and more doctrinaire minds. Thus he is apt to be cited as authority for varied and often inconsistent policies: as opposed to "entangling alliances" and as insisting that we might have to "marry ourselves to the British fleet and nation"; as favoring private enterprise and as advocating public intervention, if necessary, to secure protection from dangerous concentrations of economic power. So both New Dealers and Anti-New Dealers claim to be the "Jeffersonian Democrats" of today.

Jefferson was none the less fundamentally constant. He stood invariably for free elections, a free press, and freedom of religion; for public provision of educational opportunity; for an economic policy designed to prevent the extreme inequalities that would destroy free enterprise. In foreign relations he demanded consistently a policy that would tend to isolate the United States from the "exterminating havoc" threatening the rest of the world, but capable, when necessary, of cooperating with other states willing to throw their weight on the side of free government.

—CHARLES SEYMOUR,
President, Yale University

BASIC CONVICTIONS

JEFFERSON HELD CONVICTIONS which embodied principles not subject to the vicissitudes of transient circumstances. He maintained such convictions without fear against men who opposed them. Basic among these convictions and principles was his belief in human freedom and equality. His cure for the ills of democracy was more and purer and truer democracy. And his idea of government was minimum and not maximum abridgement of freedom, and only such abridgement of freedom as was essential to the larger liberty for each and for all. He would not deny today the duty of the whole body which we call the State to do what only the whole body can do to suppress evil and to promote well being, but he would recognize the subordination of the functions of the State to the duties which can be performed only by the individual, the family, the school and the Church.

—ROBERT E. SPEER,
*Ex-President, Federal Council of the
Churches of Christ in America*

FREEDOM TO LEARN

MORE IMPORTANT than the immediate impact of his personality upon the world of his day are certain spiritual qualities to which Thomas Jefferson gave vigorous expression and which perennially have fed the springs of thought and feeling of the proponents of democracy and liberalism from his day to this.

Jefferson himself placed greatest importance on his efforts in behalf of popular government, on his advocacy of religious freedom and on his efforts to advance popular education. Before his death, in appraisal of his own work, he asked that these words be placed upon his tomb: "Here was buried Thomas Jefferson, Author of the Declaration of Independence; of the Statute of Virginia for religious freedom; and father of the University of Virginia."

Jefferson's legacy to us is not so much his particular solution of the problem of government, but rather his conviction that the problem must be solved anew by each generation. He believed that nothing is unchangeable but the inherent and inalienable rights of man.

Were Jefferson living today, he would doubtless again assert as being self-evident truth that men should be equal in their right to life, liberty and the pursuit of happiness. The doctrines of the Nazi tyranny, subordinating man to the state, he would condemn as the antithesis of freedom and the Rights of Man.

Morover, a modern Thomas Jefferson would combat racial prejudice and religious bigotry. In season and out of season he would urge and practice tolerance, content to rest the case for or against any man, or measure, or philosophy of government upon the appeal to reason and the judgment of the majority of mankind.

For Jefferson put his trust finally and everlastingly in the wisdom of the majority of the people if given freedom to learn. He believed that freedom of conscience, free press, free discussion, free schools are the indispensable means to popular government and a free society. "Above all things I hope the education of the common people will be attended to. Educate and inform the whole mass of the people. Enable them to see that it is to their interest to preserve peace and order and they will preserve them. They are the only sure reliance for the preservation of our liberty," said Jefferson.

—J. W. STUDEBAKER,
United States Commissioner of Education

FUNDAMENTALS OF GREATNESS

THOSE OF US who enjoy the blessings of free institutions owe a great debt of gratitude to Thomas Jefferson and other brave souls of his time who saw the true meaning of Freedom and Liberty. The Declaration of Independence, the articles of Confederation, the Constitution and the Bill of Rights taken together form the great modern Magna Charta of not only American Liberty, but world freedom as well.

The influence of Jefferson was stamped in every word and every line of the Declaration of Independence. Indirectly, his personality is found in the other documents, so sacred to all Americans who appreciate the blessings of our modern instititions.

We need to be reminded that freedom was not the creation of men, it is of divine origin. Many centuries before Jefferson was born, the Ten Commandments and the Golden Rule had stamped indelibly in the laws of the world that man was free, that liberty and the rights of human personality came from God himself. They were as much the Birthright of human beings as the air, the sunrise and the soil under foot.

Jefferson's greatness is found in his recognition of the Divinity of the Freedom and rights of each human being. The poorly informed may think that freedom and liberty was the result of the Declaration of Independence and our American way of life. Jefferson proclaimed that the right to liberty, freedom and opportunity was self-evident and the divine inheritance of people everywhere. It was his program to restore the opportunity of securing, and then preserving liberty. At the same time he proposed to destroy tyrants and those in the pathway of human progress.

Today all should be familiar with the Declaration of Independence and it should be read aloud in every family and every home on the Fourth of July or at least once each year. A knowledge of our Constitution and an appreciation of our Bill of Rights should be the possession of every true American.

The story of the life of Jefferson has a startling value to us today. Some of the evils he thundered against in his youth and the prime of manhood are again creeping into government and our way of life. Change and progress bring new conditions but always, and at all times, the philosophy of Thomas Jefferson and his belief that the people are finally the source of power is just as appreciable today as it was in 1776 or the following decades when he was active in the affairs of government. Jefferson had the quiet qualities of statesmanship. He was possessed with the fundamentals of greatness, but after all, his humility, his character, his patriotism stamped him as one whose name would be forever listed among the great.

The ideals of Thomas Jefferson will live as long as freedom is cherished by the citizens of this republic.

—Louis J. Taber,
Past Master, The National Grange

THE BANNER OF JUSTICE

TWO CONTRIBUTIONS OF THOMAS JEFFERSON were essential at the founding of our national life and are essential now, his belief in the capacity of common people, and his conviction of the importance of common people and that each of them needed protection against the corruption of power.

When he wrote the Declaration of Independence and declared all men created equal, only one man among 25 men and women and children could vote; in 12 of the 13 colonies only the property holder could vote. Most who subscribed to the Declaration did not mean to include bond servants and slaves. But Jefferson possessed that almost mystical belief in the common man with all his defects which asserts that over the long pull the conclusion of all the people about what is good for them is better than the carefully thought-out plans of a few, however well intentioned. Only the wearer of the shoe knows where it pinches. Let the industrialist and the Government planner remember that daily.

Power is the great corrupter, and Jefferson, like so many of his associates in the founding of our nation, knew the many proofs of that proposition in history through the centuries. There is only one protection against power, and that is the Bill of Rights imbedded in our Constitution and National consciousness. The days of tyranny in Government were so far away in history that we had forgotten. But the stories of the Gestapo and of the Japanese military police have shocked us awake. The Bill of Rights, which is Jefferson's accomplishment almost singlehanded, can be annotated in nearly every article by events in Germany or Japan. It stands as the banner of Justice and Mercy against the bloody tyranny of East and West.

Long may the memory of Thomas Jefferson be green!

—CHARLES P. TAFT,
*Assistant Director, Office of Defense
Health and Welfare Services*

THE FOE OF TYRANNY

THIS YEAR IS THE 200TH ANNIVERSARY of the birth of Thomas Jefferson, great exponent of the rights of man, author of the Declaration of Independence, and father of the Bill of Rights in our Constitution. Always the foe of tyranny, if Thomas Jefferson were alive today he would doubtless be the author of a new Bill of Rights for all mankind.

His philosophy of human values is as valid today as it was in the Revolutionary period of our nation's development. What he led in attaining for his countrymen must now be done for the world. Technology and industry have changed the face of America since the time of Jefferson, but the freedom of the human spirit, which he espoused, remains as our dearest heritage.

Today there are four fundamental human rights that must be assured for ourselves and our posterity: civil rights, economic rights, political rights, and social rights. These basic human rights are all assumed by the American people as inalienable as the right to "life, liberty, and the pursuit of happiness".

The United Nations, in accepting the Atlantic Charter as the basis for their alliance, recognize these human rights as the primary goal of the war against modern tyranny. Practically every modern constitution, including those of Russia and China, guarantees these primary human rights, based upon the concept of the supreme value of human personality.

The Institute of International Law, on October 12, 1929, adopted a resolution which asserted: "That the juridical conscience of the civilized world demands the recognition for the individual of rights preserved from all infringement on the part of the state. . . . That it is important to extend to the entire world international recognition of the rights of man."

Thomas Jefferson, were he alive today, would be the first to agree that the rights of man can only be secured by international action. This concept was voiced for all time by John Locke, who wrote in 1689: "The state of nature has a law to govern it, which obliges everyone; and reason, which is that law, teaches all mankind, who will but consult it, as being all equal and independent, no one ought to harm another in his life, health, liberty, or possessions."

—E. Guy Talbott,
*Field Secretary, World Alliance
for International Friendship
Through the Churches*

IF JEFFEERSON LIVED TODAY

EVERY AMERICAN HONORS THOMAS JEFFERSON, the first great champion of American democracy, but far too few stop to think what Thomas Jefferson believed Democracy to be, and from which quarters he feared it might be menaced; nor do they ask themselves what he would think of American democracy today.

Mr. Jefferson believed in a society of free and self-governing men, who largely managed their own affairs, with the smallest amount of intervention by the State. He believed this was only possible when almost all men owned some form of productive wealth and no man or group of men owned or controlled sufficient to make them masters over the lives of thousands of others. He feared the centralization of Power, whether power of wealth or power of government. He feared the growth of vast cities, containing millions of propertyless, rootless proletarians. He did not believe in "masses" but in "the people". He despised demagogues and believed that Democracy must create out of the people a true aristocracy of leadership. He put the philosophical above the technical. He did not believe that labor was a commodity but that a man's skills were property, to be invested in society, not sold to the highest bidder, by collective or individual bargaining.

He believed the aim of government and economics was human welfare and development. Although he despised most churches as dogmatic societies of vested interests, he believed in God the Creator and called himself a "Deist". He had great respect for strong character and intellectual achievement and although Alexander Hamilton was his greatest political enemy, and he disagreed fundamentally with Hamilton's view of the State and Society, he admired his enemy and set up a bust of him in Monticello.

If Hamilton, however, could return to earth today, he would see his picture of America largely fullfilled. He would see an organized and largely self-sufficient continent of immense cities and tremendous industries; he would see a powerful central government assuming ever self-increasing power. He would see the larger industries and farms crowding out the smaller. He would see concentrated Power.

But if Jefferson could return, he would see his fears confirmed. He would see the yeoman and artisan pushed into the vast proletariat, and he would not be comforted by the size of their income, for he was not so concerned with income as with ownership. He would be appalled by the realization that some hundred corporations or less controlled the bulk of the productive manufacturing wealth of the country. Nor would he be in the least comforted by being told that huge trade union bodies bargained collectively with these corporations for the lives of millions of men. He would regard them as economic slaves nevertheless, and the trade unions as merely agents to obtain for their slavery a higher price.

He would look at this vast and beautiful continent, embracing every variety of climate and landscape, and containing a population still small relative to its size, and note with despair that 35 per cent of that population lived in 92 cities of over 100,000; that nearly 24 per cent lived in cities of over a quarter million; and that 12 per cent lived in five single cities of over a million.

He would see that the town meeting has all but disappeared; that political action has become largely reduced to voting for candidates picked by "machines"; that philosophy has become the stepchild of education; that security is reckoned not by ownership but by guaranteed income and state-supported insurances. He would see that Congressmen are guardians and instruments of interests, not free men and philosophers governing for the general welfare, and he would hardly find in the home of a single one of them a library equal to that which he accumulated at Monticello when America was largely wilderness.

Yes, we honor Mr. Jefferson, but we often blaspheme him in honoring him. Neither the Republican, Democratic, Socialist or Communist Parties have the right to speak in his name.

I think if Jefferson could return to us and become a political leader in the middle of our highly organized twentieth century, he would be against the whole trend of the times.

He would demand the nationalization through public corporations of all basic raw materials and natural monopolies, such as communications and utilities.

He would demand the decentralization of industries into many branches, situated in small towns through the length and breadth of the union and their transformation into cooperative undertakings.

He would break up all vast farms, prohibiting any person or corporation from owning more than a certain acreage, and plan for the organization of these smallholds into cooperatives for greater efficiency in production and marketing.

He would restore philosophy to the primary position in the universities.

He would advocate the merging of numbers of states with much greater State Rights, and in this would be immensely impressed by the example of Switzerland.

He would work to reform the tax laws, removing all penalties for the improvement of property and penalizing all speculation.

He would advocate the public purchase of all lands surrounding cities and the turning of these lands into garden allotments for city workers.

He would fight to his last breath against the maintenance of a large standing army, and advocate a militia system on the Swiss model.

He would work to abolish the proletariat.

He would be opposed by Big Business, Big Labor,

Big Farming and Big Government, all of whom would brand him as a Reactionary.

But he would be, what he always was, a revolutionary: Revolutionary for Freedom, for Independence, and for the Comman Man.

—Dorothy Thompson

DEATHLESS IDEALS

THOMAS JEFFERSON'S PHILOSOPHY OF GOVERNMENT was based on the exercise of "the common sense of the common people". He fought valiantly toward his objective—an objective which another great President called "government of the people, by the people and for the people".

Jefferson faced powerful opposition; but his principles have lived and grown, in America and elsewhere. Today a score of nations are banded together to defend the rights of man, for which he fought, against extinction by dictators seeking to enslave mankind. But the strength of the free peoples of the world, on which Jefferson relied, is making itself felt; their rights will be preserved.

More and more, in our own country, Jefferson's ideals have been applied and power has been transferred directly to the people. Our history in recent years has been dominated by a movement towards the realization of his aims.

Doubtless he would find the greatest satisfaction in the following advances toward his way of government —a few of those achieved only in the last decade!

The application of "economic democracy" in agriculture through a system of planning, controlled by the vote of the farmers themselves, by which our 30 millions of rural people assure themselves against the effects of huge surplusses, ruinously low prices, and other economic disasters.

Establishment of social security for the aged, unemployment insurance, and bank deposit insurance, through which the people assure themselves against destitution that otherwise might come with age and with business misfortunes.

Assurance of the right of the masses of working people to have power over their own affairs, freeing them of much of the undue control of their lives that once was exerted by a relatively small employing class.

Jefferson was opposed to any fixed, inflexible system of government. His view was that government and its administration must be tailored to fit the needs of a people—and retailored when those needs change. The process of change, through legislation within the Constitutional limits, has proceeded in the last decade perhaps more rapidly than ever before, to meet the rapidly changing needs of the people.

Jefferson still lives in his deathless ideals. And the world still is moving, sometimes slowly, sometimes rapidly, toward the application of the principles to which he devoted his life.

—FRANK C. WALKER,
United States Postmaster General

FOR A BETTER WORLD

THOMAS JEFFERSON, IN THE STIRRING TIMES which saw the birth of our nation, stood in the forefront of those who gave us our democratic way of life.

A gentleman in the service of Virginia, a statesman given to the study of every branch of the learning of his day, having a knowledge of French, Spanish and Italian, as well as of Latin and of Greek, no more cultivated mind, no broader experience of men and their affairs, no clearer vision, was ever brought to a higher task.

A leader in the successful movement to secure a humanitarian revision of the harsh penal code of his day, he gave to Virginia her statute for religious freedom. The founder of the University of Virginia, he was the first American statesman to give to education its true place in our free society. The author of our Declaration of Independence, he has won an outstanding place in American history for his many contributions to our country's progress, both as distinguished citizen and during his two terms as President of the United States of America.

The protection of the governed against the misuse of the powers entrusted to government was his constant concern. He saw clearly that what had been attained in the past must be preserved for a future and a better world. The preservation of ancient and accepted ways, so that they might serve to guard the human rights he had declared to be inalienable, was Jefferson's contribution to making the aspirations of his age into the living reality we have so long enjoyed.

It was Jefferson who recognized that each one of us has his own life to live, and that none can divest us of that responsibility,—that our equality in that responsibility is of such supreme importance as to carry the true meaning of human equality to all free men. It was his uncompromising faith in his fellow men that led him to place his trust in the righteous and unerring judgment of our free and sovereign people.

In this hour, when we are waging total war lest this people perish, it is the Jeffersonian tradition which has given us the vision that not only free men, but free nations also, have achieved their freedom in order that they may cooperate in preserving their heritage for the generations to come.

—THOMAS J. WATSON

CONSTRUCTIVE COURAGE

THOMAS JEFFERSON BELIEVED THAT GOVERNMENT must meet the needs of the people. That made him a revolutionary philosopher at a time when modern institutions of government were being formulated out of the failures of the past. What distinguished him above the run-of-mill reformer was the constructive courage of his practical application of the ideals to which he subscribed and for which he was so powerful an advocate.

He was not one to tear down except to clear the way for building better. He did not believe that chaos would precipitate cures. Best of all, he did not fancy that he was the only man who had all the right answers.

It seems to me that he was the sort of man who believed in a constant readiness to change when change would improve conditions. The Louisiana Purchase was an example of his readiness to face reality, even if it meant swallowing some of his own "anti-imperialist" words.

His recognition that succeeding generations might need and want to be free to change basic structures was one of the great contributions to the principle of constitutional government, even though it was essentially an underlying fact of British experience.

Those who really believe in democracy are willing to trust in the capacity of the chosen representatives of the people to find the right answers. Jefferson was one who preferred to trust the people rather than a self-constituted aristocracy.

At the same time, Jefferson believed that, once the majority had set a course, it was the obligation of all people to respect the decision. Yet as President, he had to experience the stubborn insistence of a selfish few to place their interests above the needs and policy of the nation. Even he found his management of the general welfare embarrassed by those who preferred the profits of unrestricted trade above the interests of the nation.

Thomas Jefferson was one of those who created our birthright of freedom and who gave substance to the dignity of the common man. He was a true founder not merely of the American system of representative democracy but also of the American way of life.

The working men and women of America owe to him far more than we usually realize because he earmarked for the common people the determination of their own conditions of life.

—ROBERT J. WATT,
International Representative
American Federation of Labor

GUIDE TO THE FUTURE

HISTORY (OR A SIGNIFICANT PART OF IT) has a curious way of repeating itself. Almost all the problems of the present and of the future were once problems of the past—whether they were solved or left unanswered. We are today paying tribute to the memory of Thomas Jefferson. And we are doing this not because his career represents merely a chapter in the struggle for human liberty. His wisdom and his yearnings for freedom are as fresh and vital as they were the day he eloquently urged them upon his countrymen. And this, it seems to me, is the best test of the right of a man's reputation to survive. Jefferson faced situations and problems that we are facing now. Perhaps a few of his answers will demonstrate why his reputation has grown with the years.

We are discussing compulsory military training as a permanent feature of our national life. Jefferson said: "We must adopt a system of military duty (that of classing the militia according to age and allotting each age to the particular kind of service to which it is competent). We must adopt it now and all will be safe. We had in the United States in 1805, in round numbers of free, able-bodied men, in all, 720,000 of the ages 18 to

45 inclusive. With this properly classified, organized, trained, armed and subject to tours of a year of military duty, we have no more to fear for the defense of our country. We must train and classify the whole of our male citizens and make military instruction a regular part of collegiate education."

Are not his words about the "swarms of northern [European] barbarians" and the "conquering ruffians" applicable to the Nazi legions of this day — and to America's place in the great array of United Nations? Jefferson said: "Should the cloud of barbarism and despotism again obscure the science and liberties of Europe, this country remains to preserve and restore light and liberty to them. In short, the flames kindled on the 4th of July, 1776, have spread over too much of the globe to be extinguished by the feeble engines of despotism; on the contrary, they will consume these engines and all who work them."

Mighty Brazil has joined the United Nations in the struggle against Fascism, but Jefferson longed for it many years ago: "I should rejoice to see the fleets of Brazil and the United States riding together as brethren of the same family and having the same interests."

He foresaw "total war" and advised the only means of meeting it. He said that during the total war in Europe "our country will require the union of all its friends to resist its enemies within and without ... The last hope of human liberty in this world rests on us. We ought, for so dear a state, to sacrifice every attachment and every enmity. Leave the President free to

137

choose his own coadjutors, to pursue his own measures, and support him and them, even if we think we are wiser than they, honester than they are, or possessing more enlarged information of the state of things. If we move in mass, be it ever so circuitously, we shall attain our object; but if we break into squads, every one pursuing the path he thinks most direct, we become an easy conquest to those who can now barely hold us in check."

Jefferson's wisdom is a precious part of the heritage of the past. It vindicates itself today and gives us a certain guide to the future. As long as we love liberty and are determined to preserve it we shall honor Thomas Jefferson.

—GROVER A. WHALEN

WISDOM AND VISION

APPLICABILITY TO THE CONTEMPORARY SCENE of much
which Thomas Jefferson wrote and said strikes one
with uncanny force today. Particularly is this true with
respect to the moral and physical harm human slavery
does to slave and slaveholder alike at this time when
Hitler and Hirohito fight to enslave the entire world.
Today when the problem of race and color becomes
visible to the majority of Americans for the first time
as a global instead of only a national or sectional one
we see how Jefferson was infinitely wise. And we see too
how wise we would have been—ourselves as well as our
ancestors—had we listened to him, especially when a
single vote or the votes of small blocs in Congress or
Parliament, motivated by selfishness or ignorance or
chauvinism may wreak as great harm to us all as did
that one vote about which Jefferson wrote M. de Meu-
nier in 1786 regarding slavery in the Western territory.
"There were ten states present," Jefferson wrote, "six
voted unanimously for it, three against it, and one was
divided; and seven votes being requisite to decide the
proposition affirmatively, it was lost. The voice of a
single individual of the State which was divided, or of
one of those which was negative, would have prevented

this abominable crime from spreading over the new country. Thus we see the fate of millions unborn hanging on the tongue of one man, and Heaven was silent in that awful moment!"]

And when in 1943 we see a reactionary coalition of Republicans and Democrats, Northerners and Southerners, desperately fighting to turn back the clock of progress in its movement towards a juster and saner world, we find history repeating itself and Jefferson again accurately diagnosing and fighting for the right. For thus he wrote in his Autobiography the story of how the abolition of slavery, destined to plague the United States for generations and even to this day, was elided from the text of the Declaration of Independence; "The clause . . . reprobating the enslaving of the inhabitants of Africa was struck out in complaisance to South Carolina and Georgia, who had never attempted to restrain the importation of slaves, and who, on the contrary, still wish to continue it. Our Northern brethren also, I believe, felt a little tender under those censures; for though their people had very few slaves themselves yet they had been pretty considerable carriers of them to others."

Nor is their lacking disturbing consciousness of what is going on today in India and Burma and Africa and the West Indies as well as in our own country when we read Jefferson's message to the House of Burgesses in 1774, "The abolition of domestic slavery is the great object of desire in those colonies. . . . But previous to the enfranchisement of the slaves we have, it is necessary to exclude all further importations from Africa. Yet our repeated attempts to effect this by prohibitions . . . have been defeated by his Majesty's negative; thus preferring the immediate advantages of a few British corsairs to the lasting interests of the American states, and to the rights of human nature, deeply wounded by this infamous practice."

Have we, 169 years later, attained Jefferson's wisdom and vision? One wonders.

—WALTER WHITE,
Secretary, National Association
for the Advancement
of Colored People

RE-DEDICATE AMERICA
TO JEFFERSON

THOMAS JEFFERSON'S IS THE THIRD of the great bi-centenaries. First Franklin, then Washington, and now Jefferson—the three great pioneers and liberators of the American Democracy. It would not do to say that Jefferson was the greatest of all. But Jefferson was as much as any man the political and spiritual creator of the American Republic.

Any one of the three references on the gravestone of Thomas Jefferson would have sufficed to give him immortality; the conjuncture of the three guarantees his deathless fame. The glory of Jefferson lies in his timelessness. His words and works are as if he lived beyond the limitations of time and dealt in immortal fashion with eternal things.

To have been in the course of his life the author of the Declaration of Independence and the Bill of Rights is to have anticipated the Atlantic Charter, to have envisaged the Four Freedoms, to have enrolled himself with the United Nations as against the Axis powers. These would have destroyed the two Documents, which are the priceless heritage of free men and of all men who would be free.

Let our country pause on the Jefferson bi-centenary —not to do homage to the man, whose name is beyond praise or homage, but to re-dedicate itself to the principles which he was first to enunciate, and to the ideals by which he forever enriched the Western World, and, under God, it may yet be all the sons and daughters of man.

—STEPHEN S. WISE,
President, American Jewish Congress

INDEX OF CONTRIBUTORS